‹ The Book

BEER
AWESOMENESS

A Champion's Guide to
PARTY SKILLS, AMAZING BEER ACTIVITIES,
AND MORE THAN FORTY DRINKING GAMES

Written by BEN APPLEBAUM *and* DAN DISORBO

Illustrations by DAN DISORBO

CHRONICLE BOOKS
SAN FRANCISCO

Library of Congress Cataloging-in-Publication Data is available.

ISBN 978-1-4521-0501-7

Manufactured in China

Based on the design by Andrew Schapiro
Typeset by DC Type
Typeset in Hoefler, Knockout, and Brothers

10 9 8 7 6 5 4 3 2 1

Chronicle Books LLC
680 Second Street
San Francisco, California 94107
www.chroniclebooks.com

TABLE OF
Awesomeness

INTRODUCTION

BEAUTY
IS IN THE HAND OF THE
BEER HOLDER

BEER IS perhaps mankind's single greatest concoction and the most widely consumed beverage on the planet (besides water and tea). Yet the true art of beer drinking and its related activities have somehow remained largely ignored throughout beer's hazy history.

How is it possible that everyone's favorite pastime has received so little formal coverage? How can so few Americans identify what style of beer they are drinking? When will formal chugging techniques become required learning for all adults? Why do we so rarely learn the proper rules of beer-drinking games?

It is time to treat throwing back a few brew-ha-has with significance, gravitas, and other impressive words befitting such an important act. From pouring to storing, from crushing cans to keg stands, from beer bongs to beer pong, we've created this guide to help you develop the skills you'll need to master the awesomeness of beer.

"But is beer drinking really that important?" you ask.

"Hell yeah, it is," we answer.

"Prove it," you retort.

Simply put: beer drinking is just good for you.

Beer does your body good. This magical bread soup has been a significant nutritional staple for generations. Only recently in human history has it been considered a luxury. A myriad of studies prove its health benefits. Don't trust us? Check out a little thing called the Internet, it's full of facts.

BEER DOES YOUR MIND GOOD TOO. While we delve more into the physical benefits later in the book, we must also stress the psychological importance of proper beer drinking. Beer offers a mindfulness and awareness that breaks us out of our autopilot daily routines. How do you think Buddha got such a prodigious Buddha belly?

Beer does our society good. Beer drinking represents the perfect antidote to the harried pace and isolation of modern life. While technology is pushing us toward shallow social media friendships, beer drinking is pulling us back to reality. So even when the day comes that you can download your virtual date, you will need to meet up with a real, live human to hoist a hefeweizen.

Beer is also deliciously inefficient. It's the original slow food. Brewing beer was and will always be part science and part art. And drinking beer, the right way, is no different. It requires a combination of practice, knowledge, and cultural reinforcement. You aren't born knowing how to open a beer bottle with your teeth. You need to learn it.

But most of this drinking knowledge has been shared informally—passed down through cultures by simple word of mouth. And in our expert opinion, that's not good enough. Don't get us wrong, we believe in the oral tradition. And we believe it's perfect for sharing mythology, spirituality, and family values. What we call the little stuff. Beer drinking, however, is simply too important to risk its integrity on something so unofficial.

So we have endeavored to put into words what we all love to put into our bellies: beer and all of its awesomeness.

And in true beer-drinking tradition, let's begin this journey with a toast.

May the knowledge about to be bestowed upon you forever help make you a beer-drinking champion.

Cheers!

BEER BANTER

"He was a wise man who invented beer."
—PLATO

CHAPTER

1

BREW
SCHOOL

You need to know it to own it.

AND BY "IT" WE MEAN BEER, and by "own" we mean becoming a skilled practitioner of the art and science of drinking "it." And that's where we will begin.

Understanding the history of beer, the fundamentals of brewing, and the basic taxonomy of the various forms is not just for random trivia nights or boring your buddies to death. No, we believe that this is the foundation on which to build your beer-drinking skills. Respect the knowledge of the past because we are all just drinking on the shoulders of giants. Please don't spill.

The Basics of Beer

FIRST THINGS THIRST, let's define exactly what you will be devoting every waking minute—and several non-waking ones—to perfecting.

Beer is the world's oldest and most popular alcoholic beverage, an incredible feat for such a complicated, temperamental, and polarizing liquid. It's also testament to its otherworldly powers, surprisingly nutritional benefits, and significant economic influence.

All of this from a fermentation of partially germinated grains flavored with dried flowers. While it doesn't sound impressive—or particularly masculine—it has had a significant role in our history.

BEER BANTER

"From man's sweat and God's love, beer came into the world."
—SAINT ARNOLD OF METZ
Patron saint of brewers

DRINKER DICTIONARY
BEER SYNONYMS

Amber fluid	Cold one	Keg innards	Silly seltzer
Barley juice	Cold water sandwich	Libation	Social lubricant
Bomber	Coldie	Liquid bread	Suds
Brain hammer	Daddy's milk	Liquid gold	Swill
Brew	Frosty	Loudmouth soup	Swipe
Brewdog	Giggle water	Malt beverage	Time travel in a bottle
Brew-ha-ha	Gold elixir	Nectar of the gods	Tinnie
Brewski	Grog	Oat soda	Tummy buster
Cerveza	Gutter-ade	Old horizontal	Wallop
Chugger's delight	Hop juice	Post-party cologne	Wheat treat
Codswallop	Hoppy happiness	Reeb	Wobbly pops

A Brief History of Beer

SO, HOW DID BEER COME ABOUT? It's a question that is as old as time itself. Fermentation happens naturally in fruit, courtesy of wild yeasts. Some animals have been known to partake of a little spiked fruit—and early humans were likely not far behind. This theory would explain the creation of wine and other fruity drinks. But beer is different.

Grains don't share the same easily fermenting properties. They need some hot enzyme action to convert the plant's starches into soluble sugars. And those enzymes come from two sources: saliva or partial germination. Either way, the path to the first brew was neither easy nor peasy.

But it happened. Somehow the grains—possibly through a storage snafu—were soaked and dried and soaked again. Then they came to float in some water and were left to rot. And it was good. Real good.

BREW FACT

The earliest brewers were women. High priestesses were divinely inspired to brew it by their culture's goddesses: Ninkasi (Sumerian), Ceres (Roman), and Elvira (American).

Some of the earliest records of beer consumption come from as far back as 4200 B.C.E., found on Babylonian clay tablets featuring detailed beer recipes. The Babylonians weren't the only ones getting their drink on, however; other societies, such as the Assyrians, the Egyptians, and the Chinese have all been reported to be massive beer heads.

THE WORLD'S LONGEST BEER RUN

9500 B.C.E.: Neolithic farmers cultivate cereals and possibly a buzz.

4200 B.C.E.: Babylonians carve beer recipes into clay tablets.

2300 B.C.E.: The Chinese brew their version of beer, *kiu*.

1600 B.C.E.: Egyptian texts contain medicinal uses for beer.

55 B.C.E.: The Romans introduce their form of beer to Northern Europe.

500 C.E.: Europe graduates from smaller home brewing to brewing beer on a large scale in monasteries.

1200: Beer making is firmly established as a commercial enterprise in Germany, Austria, and England.

1492: Columbus finds Indians making beer from corn and black birch sap.

1516: William IV, Duke of Bavaria, adopts the *Reinheitsgebot* (purity law), according to which the only allowed ingredients of beer are water, hops, and barley malt.

1602: Dr. Alexander Nowell discovers that ale can be stored longer in cork-sealed glass bottles.

1663: America's first brewery opens in lovely Hoboken, New Jersey.

1820: The Industrial Revolution introduces technology and practices that take beer brewing into mass production.

1876: Louis Pasteur develops a process to stabilize beers twenty-two years before it's applied to milk.

1891: American inventor William Painter creates the crown cap.

1919: The Eighteenth Amendment is ratified, marking the beginning of Prohibition.

1933: Prohibition is repealed, thankfully.

1935: The beer can is introduced.

1978: President Jimmy Carter revokes the federal tax on home beer brewers, which sparks a craft beer revival in the United States.

2010: An estimated 196 million barrels of beer are produced in the United States (1 barrel = 31 gallons of beer).

RIGHT NOW: *The Book of Beer Awesomeness* is being read by a very smart person. (Psst, that means you.)

BEER DRINKING THROUGHOUT HISTORY

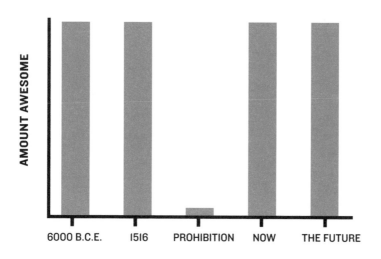

AMOUNT AWESOME

6000 B.C.E.   1516   PROHIBITION   NOW   THE FUTURE

Beer's Building Blocks

BEER BREWING HAS EVOLVED into a complex procedure that has been said to require both art and science. Of course, in reality, neither art nor science is an actual ingredient. However, the following components are:

WATER

WHAT IT IS: Two parts hydrogen, one part oxygen, it's the stuff that makes up most of the Earth, most of the human body and, not surprisingly, most of beer.

WHAT IT DOES FOR BEER: More than 90 percent of the finished product consists of this one ingredient, so though it may not seem like anything special, water (and the quality of water used) is a crucial factor in beer making.

DIFFERENT TYPES: What makes the water important is its mineral content. When dealing with beer, the kind of water used comes in two major types: hard and soft. For example, Dublin has hard water well suited to making stout, such as Guinness; while the Czech Republic has soft water well suited to making pale lager, such as Pilsner Urquell.

BARLEY

WHAT IT IS: Barley is a cereal grain, not unlike wheat or oats. Barley is like your slacker brother: it's terrible at its job as a baking grain. Also like your slacker brother, barley has one thing it is incredible at doing, and it's not playing "Rock Band," but making sugars that convert into alcohol.

WHAT IT DOES FOR BEER: Barley's purpose in beer can be summed up by a word: ~~Awesome~~ malting. Malting occurs when barley is soaked and drained to activate the germination of the plant from the seed. This activates enzymes that convert starch reserves and proteins into sugars and amino acids. Once the seeds sprout, the grain is dried in a kiln to stop the enzymes until it's time to brew.

BREW FACT

"How important is water quality to brewing? In the early 1800s, pale ales were all the rage in London. A small brewer in Burton by the name of Samuel Allsopp decided to copy the style, and the London boozehounds loved it. This was due to the water—the hills around Burton were (and are) full of gypsum, a sulfate that brings out the bitter flavors from the hops during the brewing process.

The English beer drinkers demanded ales from Burton seemingly above all others, starting a beer gold rush. Eventually, chemists discovered the secret of the water, and breweries elsewhere simply added sulfate to copy the effect—a process known as 'Burtonisation.' "
—RICHARD TAYLOR
Beer expert and host of TheBeerCast.com

DIFFERENT TYPES: Barley comes in a variety of types, distinguished by the number of seeds on the stalk of the plant. European brewers prefer the two-row type because it malts best and has a higher starch-to-husk ratio. American brewers often go with the six-row type because it's cheaper to grow and contains a higher concentration of the enzymes.

YEAST

WHAT IT IS: Yeast is a single-celled microorganism that reproduces asexually through the less-than-sexy budding process. Classified as fungi, there are hundreds of strains of yeast currently identified. The strain of yeast that has been commonly used in baking and beer fermentation for thousands of years is called *Saccharomyces cerevisiae.* (Hint: baby name idea!)

WHAT IT DOES FOR BEER: Yeast brings the brew to the fermentation process, which causes the malt in the beer to magically transform into an alcoholic beverage. Yeast can also have an impact on the brew's final aromas and flavors.

DIFFERENT TYPES: There are two important kinds of the *Saccharomyces cerevisiae* strain of yeast to remember: top-fermenting yeast and bottom-fermenting yeast.

Top-fermenting yeast is called such because the top of the wort foams up when using this type of yeast. Also known as "ale yeast," it ferments at a higher temperature (68°F–72°F). Conversely, bottom-fermenting yeast, or "lager yeast," ferments at lower temperatures (48°F–52°F).

HOPS

WHAT IT IS: Hops are budding flowers that are added to the boil (see page 20) to give beer its signature taste. Hops are also a kissing cousin to everyone's favorite plant—cannabis.

WHAT IT DOES FOR BEER: Hops essentially "flavor" the beer, contributing heavily to its aroma, bitterness, and finish. They also allow the yeast to ferment more efficiently. The amount added ultimately affects the "spiciness" and fullness of the beer's taste. Hops can also function as a natural preservative for beer.

DIFFERENT TYPES: There are two basic kinds of hops: bittering (or "noble") hops and flavoring (or "aroma") hops. How the hops are used and when they're brought into the brewing process change the outcome of the beer.

AND THE OTHER STUFF—EXTRA STUFF THAT MAKES BEER EXTRA SPECIAL

WHEAT:

A main ingredient in, you guessed it, wheat beers. Gives a crisp, refreshing taste and can help retain the head as well.

RICE:

Rice is added because it's cheaper than using all barley for brewing—hence the beers that have rice as an adjunct are cheaper and usually mass-produced.

SPICES:

Before hops became the primary flavoring agent, spices were used to provide a beer with its flavor profile. Today, many

HOW BEER IS ACTUALLY MADE

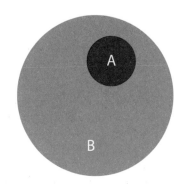

■ INGREDIENTS   ■ DIVINE INTERVENTION

BEER BY THE GLANCE

•••••••••••••••••

According to the USDA National Nutrient Database, one 12-ounce serving of regular beer has the following nutrients:

Serving Size: 12 Ounces

Amount Per Serving
Cholesterol 0 g
Fat 0 g
Calories 153
Protein 1.64 g
Carbohydrates 12.64 g
Calcium 14 mg
Magnesium 21 mg
Phosphorus 50 mg
Potassium 96 mg
Sodium 14 mg
Zinc 0.04 mg
Thiamin 0.018 mg
Riboflavin 0.089 mg
Niacin 1.826 mg
Pantothenic acid 0.146 mg
Vitamin B_6 0.164 mg

beers—such as seasonal winter, summer, and autumn brews—still rely on dried spices (like cinnamon, cloves, nutmeg, coriander, and even some variations of dried flowers) to give the brew its specific profile.

FRUIT:

While it's not a necessity in most beers, many styles are largely dependent on fruit. Some brews incorporate fruit syrup in the fermenting process while others simply use fruit extract at the end to heighten certain flavor notes.

WEIRD STUFF:

Sometimes it goes right, like with vegetables (pumpkin) and other grains (oatmeal). Sometimes it doesn't, like with garlic and liver (both used to varying degrees of disgust).

The Reality of Brewing

Like making Easy Mac and Cheese, brewing beer is a science. Unlike Easy Mac, it's painstaking work that involves several intricate steps, each of which must be executed with precision. Here's a basic look at the beer brewing process.

1. MASHING: First, grain is milled and malted, then mixed with water. The mixture is heated to allow enzymes to break the starch in the grain down into sugars.

2. LAUTERING: This is the filtration process that collects the extracts from the mashed grain.

3. BOILING: Those extracts make what's called wort. Hops are added, and the mixture is boiled to stabilize flavors and aromas.

4. WHIRLPOOLING: At the end of the boil, the wort is set into a whirlpool, which collects any solid waste (like spent hops).

5. COOLING: Next, the wort is cooled down so that yeast can be added for fermentation.

6. FERMENTING: Yeast is added to the cooled wort, causing the sugars from the malt to metabolize into alcohol and carbon dioxide.

7. MATURING: The beer settles down, allowing the fermented yeast to drift to the bottom of the tank. The beer is cooled below freezing to maintain smoothness and stored under pressure to keep it from going flat.

8. FILTERING: The beer is filtered once more to remove any remaining yeast and hop particles. Not all beer is filtered.

9. PACKAGING: Finally, the beer is sealed into bottles, cans, kegs, etc., and sent out to make the world a better place.

Styles of Beer

THE NUMBER OF BEERS AVAILABLE seems as vast and varied as ESPN channels, but the truth is that there are two main types of beer out there: ales and lagers.

BEER BANTER

"A quart of ale is a dish for a king."
—WILLIAM SHAKESPEARE

ALES

Ales are old school, really old school. This original style of beer is the result of a warmer top-fermentation process that releases chemicals called esters, which have an impact on the ale's complex, full-bodied taste and rich darker colors. Ales are a bit like black-and-white movies: loved by aficionados, not always appreciated by the masses.

EXAMPLES

ENGLISH BITTER ALE

This style of ale was developed for the drinker who likes his beer with a bitter kick, hence the name. The bitterness come from a heavier dosage of hops. The final color is often akin to copper and the taste and body are usually mild with a light alcohol content. (Brands: Anchor Small Beer, Fuller's Chiswick Bitter)

PALE ALE

A popular beer internationally, the recipe for pale ales has been adapted by whichever region it's brewed in, leaving a lot of room for variation. For example, India pale ales (IPA) were brewed to be high in hops and alcohol to survive long sea journeys from England to, you guessed it, India. American pale ales and Irish red ales often contain fewer hops and less alcohol so they are considered more sessionable—a cooler word for drinkable. (Brands: Dogfish Head 60 Minute IPA, Sierra Nevada Pale Ale, Smithwick's Irish Ale)

BREW FACT

The world's strongest and most expensive beer is a blond Belgian ale. This super-strong brew is 55 percent alcohol and carries a $765 price tag per bottle. It's called "The End of History."

PORTER

Porters, originally, were a grab bag of beers thrown together by porters who worked in Victorian England. The brew we now know as a porter is essentially created to mimic their dark, full body and balanced bitterness, which is sometimes flavored with chocolate or coffee. (Brands: Blackhook Porter, Samuel Smith's Taddy Porter)

STOUT

Stout is a variation of porter made from dark roasted barley as opposed to malted barley, which gives it something of a "burnt" taste and a higher alcohol content. Stout is considered a very intense beer as far as aroma, flavor, and body are concerned. (Brands: Guinness Draught, Rogue Shakespeare Oatmeal Stout)

WHEAT ALE

Wheat ale, as its name suggests, is brewed using wheat malt. It's also fermented using a neutral yeast, giving the beer a cleaner finish. The final result is a crisper beer with light to moderate body, a wide range of bitterness, and sometimes a bit of fruity flavor. (Brands: New Belgium Sunshine Wheat, Brooklyn Summer Ale)

LAMBIC

A unique brew, lambic ale incorporates fruit and/or fruit syrup into the brewing process. The end result has low hop and malt flavors that weave into the zest provided by the potent fruits. Lambics can be made with a variety of fruits. Most lambics weigh in on the lower end of the alcohol content scale. (Brands: Lindemans Framboise Lambic, Mort Subite Kriek)

BREW FACT

"True lambics are brewed with only naturally occurring yeasts. The yeasts just float in on the breeze overnight and make the magic happen."
—RICHARD TAYLOR
Beer expert and host of TheBeerCast.com

LAGERS

Lagers, in many ways, are the polar opposite of ales: newer, cooler, sexier. Lagers are brewed at a lower temperature with bottom-fermenting yeast for a longer time. Where ales gather much of their flavor profile from the fermentation process, lagers get much of their flavor from the hops and malts. Lagers offer a much cleaner, crisper flavor and finish than the more complex ales.

Which of the following are obscure
beer varieties and which are
J. R. R. Tolkien characters?
Braggot
Dubbel
Faro
Flanders Oud Bruin
Happoshu
Kvass
Sahti

Answer: All are real beers.
Sorry, nerds.

EXAMPLES

AMERICAN LAGER

The most common type of beer in the United States, the American lager is made for the people. The pale-bodied, ultra-crisp beer is mass-produced using adjunct cereal grains like rice and corn to deliver a taste with very low bitters and minimal malt. (Brands: Miller Genuine Draft, Budweiser)

PILSNER

Pilsner is very similar to American lager with its light golden color. The difference between the two, however, lies in pilsner's heavier hop usage, which delivers a more bitter bite. Pilsners also tend to have a zestier, spicier finish. (Brands: Pilsner Urquell, St. Pauli Girl, Beck's)

BOCK

Bocks are stronger than the average lager, thanks to its jacked-up malt content. The extra step yields a very robust and potent lager with a higher alcohol punch. (Brands: Shiner Bock, Einbecker Ur-Bock, Michelob Amber Bock)

MÄRZEN (OKTOBERFEST)

As the name implies, Märzen is the lager style traditionally served up at the famous Oktoberfest in Germany. Originally, Märzen was brewed in March and left in cold storage until the fall to create a very full-bodied, copper-colored beer that's a bit high in alcohol and a perfect complement to lederhosen. (Brands: Sam Adams Oktoberfest, Victory Festbier, Spaten Oktoberfestbier Ur-Märzen)

BREW FACT

Bia Hoi, a beer found in Hanoi, is the world's cheapest beer. Described as having the appearance and flavor of Miller Lite, twelve ounces can be purchased for the equivalent of about sixteen U.S. cents.

RICE LAGER

Similar to American lagers, this specialty from Asia uses heavy amounts of rice instead of barley to create a rounded flavor experience with moderate bitterness. Rice lagers are also notorious for their dry finish. (Brands: Sapporo, Kirin)

DISTANT COUSINS

BARLEY WINE

It is called a barley *wine* because it can be as strong as wine; but since it is made from grain rather than fruit, it is, in fact, a beer. A barley wine typically reaches an alcohol strength of 8 to 12 percent by volume. This isn't a sip-with-your-pinkie-out type of hooch.

NIGHT OF THE LIVING BEER

....

"Live" beer is a term commonly used among brewers. Contrary to what the name implies, it is not beer that is gaining sentience in order to attack its thirsty overlords (i.e. you). It's actually unpasteurized, unfiltered beer that has been bottled with live yeast.

This gives the brew a chance to age and develop differently than it might during the conventional process. Sealing in the live yeast prevents oxidation and allows the yeast to break down slowly in the bottle. This second fermentation process gives the brew a more complex flavor and profile.

A BEER A DAY KEEPS THE DOCTOR AWAY: THE HEALTH BENEFITS OF BEER

....

Aside from being one of the best activities one can do with a bent elbow, drinking beer can also lead to a healthier lifestyle.

Research has shown that daily alcohol consumption can prevent heart failure. A study from Emory University tested 2,200 elderly men and women to discover that the ones who consumed 1.5 alcoholic beverages a day reduced their chances of heart failure by 50 percent. Furthermore, another study conducted by Germany, France, and the United Kingdom showed that moderate consumption of beer can have an anti-inflammatory effect on the drinker, thus lowering the risk of coronary heart disease.

Beer is good for the brain, too. Recently, scientists in Boston discovered that light (one to six drinks a week) to moderate drinkers (seven to fourteen drinks a week) have fewer strokes than non-drinkers, thanks to the way alcohol thins the blood, which can prevent the formation of clots in the brain.

BEER BY THE GLANCE

••••••••••••••••

Alcohol by volume (ABV) is a measurement that determines how much of the total volume of the beer is alcohol (duh). Here's a quick breakdown of how certain styles compare.

ALES
Bitter: 3.0%–5.8%
India pale ale (IPA): 5.0%–10.5%
Lambic: 5.0%–7.0%
Pale ale: 4.5%–5.5%
Porter: 4.5%–6.0%
Stout (imperial): 7.0%–12.0%
Wheat beer: 4.9%–5.5%

LAGERS
American lager: 4.0%–6.0%
Pilsner: 4.3%–6.0%
Bock: 6.0%–7.5%
Rice lager: 4.0%–5.5%
Märzen: 4.0%–7.0%

ICE BEER
Ice beer is a marketing term for pale lager beer brands that have undergone some degree of fractional freezing similar to the German eisbock, increasing the alcohol content. Like great comedians, this too comes from Canada, originating with Molson Ice.

MALT LIQUOR
In legal statutes, malt liquor is defined as any alcoholic beverage above or equal to 5 percent alcohol by volume made with malted barley but also containing sugar, corn, and possibly less benign ingredients. When it comes to malt liquor, quantity beats quality.

MALTERNATIVES
As the name suggests, malternatives share a malting and fermenting procedure with beer, but that's where the similarities end. The product is devoid of hops and bitters. So while these share some technical connection with beer, this side of the family tree is no longer on speaking terms with the main branch. (Brands: Smirnoff Ice, Mike's Hard Lemonade)

BREW FACT

Beer contains zero fat and actually has fewer calories than wine. A pint of beer contains about two hundred calories. The same volume of wine contains nearly four hundred calories.

The Beer Brewer Landscape

KNOWING WHERE YOUR BEER COMES FROM is like knowing where babies come from. You might be fascinated, confused, or possibly disgusted.

MACROBREWERS

Big, international brewing behemoths. They typically brew in the millions of barrels. Consistency is king. Think Budweiser, Coors, Miller.

MICROBREWERS

The maximum amount of beer a brewery can produce and still be classified as a microbrewery varies by region and by authority, though it's usually around 15,000 barrels.

TRAPPIST MONK BREWERIES

There are only seven Trappist monasteries (six in Belgium and one in the Netherlands) that produce ales under the control of these super-cool monks. Enkel, Dubbel, and Tripel are some of the types of beers they produce, but brands like Chimay and Orval might sound a bit more familiar.

BREW FACT

Patersbier translates to "fathers' beer" and is only available within the confines of the Trappist monasteries. *Patersbier* is only offered to the brothers on festive occasions, adding yet another level of exclusivity to this rare brew.

CRAFT BREWERS

Craft brewers use no adjuncts and focus more on beer styles than mass appeal. However, a craft beer can technically be manufactured by a macrobrewery as well. The American Brewers Association redefined its definition of a craft brewery to include breweries that produce up to six million U.S. beer barrels (186,000,000 U.S. gallons) a year.

FAUX CRAFT BREWERS

This is when a big guy tries to keep its connection to a so-called craft beer on the DL. Like Blue Moon, which is actually owned by Coors.

CONTRACT BREWERS

These are the ghostwriters of brewing. Some beer companies outsource the actual production of the liquid to other facilities. So your favorite Boston beer may be made in Pittsburgh, or worse, Cincinnati.

NANOBREWERS

A nanobrewery is a very small brewery operation, generally producing less than four U.S. beer barrels a year. These are often soon-to-be microbrewers in the, um, brewing.

BREWPUB

A brewpub brews and sells beer on the premises. According to the American Brewers Association, a brewpub may also be known as a "microbrewery" if its off-site beer sales exceed 75 percent of its total production.

HOME BREWER

A dude, a few tubes, and some boiling stuff. Home brewing is the land of DIY hobbyists.

The Beer Drinker Landscape

While all beer drinkers share an overall love of beer, their preferences and rituals differ greatly. Use this guide to navigate through the complicated jungle that is the beer drinker landscape.

EXHIBIT A: THE HOP HEAD

He knows a lot about beer, and he knows he knows a lot about beer. Something of a snob, the Hop Head prefers beers on the hoppier, heavier, and more challenging side and refuses to drink anything mass-produced or ever heard of before.

HOP HEAD

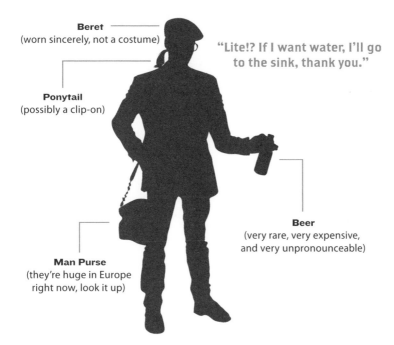

Beret
(worn sincerely, not a costume)

"Lite!? If I want water, I'll go to the sink, thank you."

Ponytail
(possibly a clip-on)

Beer
(very rare, very expensive, and very unpronounceable)

Man Purse
(they're huge in Europe right now, look it up)

EXHIBIT B: HOME BREW NERD

Not content with what's available on the shelves, the Home Brew Nerd took matters into his own hands, bought a home brewing kit, and hasn't shut up about it since. His special brews are unique and beautiful, like a Bob Ross painting; however, nobody ever seems to truly appreciate them, like a Bob Ross painting.

HOME BREW NERD

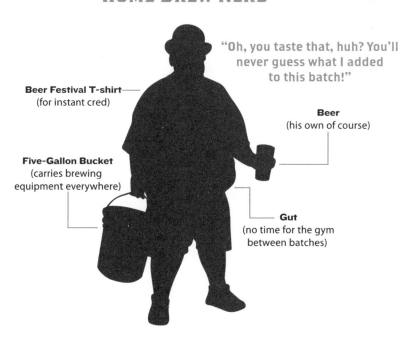

"Oh, you taste that, huh? You'll never guess what I added to this batch!"

Beer Festival T-shirt
(for instant cred)

Beer
(his own of course)

Five-Gallon Bucket
(carries brewing
equipment everywhere)

Gut
(no time for the gym
between batches)

EXHIBIT C: THE BREW BRO

Most commonly found at tailgates, keggers, and frat parties, the Brew Bro is just happy to have a fermented beverage in his hand. Though he's not picky with his preferences, he's not adventurous either, often sticking to macrobrews and chest bumps.

BREW BRO

Faded College Cap
(gotta support the team, bro)

"How much for a cup, bro..."

Beer
(whatever's in the keg, bro)

Ironic T-shirt
(instant convo
with the ladies, bro)

Flip-Flops
(shoes are so not chill, bro)

EXHIBIT D: BREW COLLAR DRINKER

The Brew Collar Drinker isn't officially done with his workday until he's popped open a cold one. A creature of habit, the Brew Collar Drinker sticks with the same thing he's been drinking for the past twenty-five years: most likely a pale lager brewed right here in 'Merica.

BREW COLLAR DRINKER

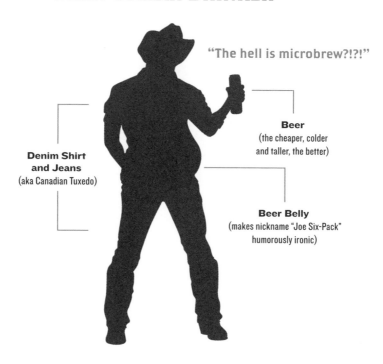

"The hell is microbrew?!?!"

Beer
(the cheaper, colder
and taller, the better)

**Denim Shirt
and Jeans**
(aka Canadian Tuxedo)

Beer Belly
(makes nickname "Joe Six-Pack"
humorously ironic)

EXHIBIT E: BREW BABE

This drinker appreciates beer for what it is . . . and not just what it does. She actually has an opinion on what she drinks. And everyone wants to hear it. She's been to Oktoberfest, done sake bombs with Japanese businessmen, and has been hit on by the most interesting man in the world.

BREW BABE

Windswept Hair
(even indoors)

"So I was traveling in a remote part of . . ."

Business Card
(letterpressed with just three words: "I'll Call You")

Beer
(always free, just because)

Designer Heels
(better to break hearts with)

BEER BANTER

"I work until beer o'clock."
—STEPHEN KING

CHAPTER

2

BEERAPHERNALIA

Never drink alone.

ANY EXPERT BEER DRINKER KNOWS that cupped hands are not enough to properly enjoy a brewski. You need more stuff to carry, cool, and care for it. A thorough knowledge and understanding of this stuff is what separates a rookie from a rock star, a dilettante from a connoisseur, a . . . you get the idea.

To become a champion beer drinker, you need to understand how the beer flows from the brewery to the belly. You need to learn which glasses bring out the best in different beers. You must master the mixology of beer-based drinks. But ultimately, you need to look like you can handle your business.

We hope this chapter can help you do just that.

Beer Containers

AS PERFECT AS BEER IS, it's still restrained by the merciless laws of gravity and physics. As a liquid, it's a malleable (and delicious) form that needs some sort of container in order to be properly held (and coddled).

CASKS

Casks are tightly sealed containers made of wooden planks reinforced by iron rings. Yes, a cask is basically a fancy word for "barrel." But it's also the traditional vessel to transport and age the brew.

PROS: Contributes to the taste and aroma of the beer; cool and old school.
CON: A short, temperamental shelf life.

BREW FACT

"Casks are not stored under pressure so they have to settle once delivered to the pub, to allow the yeast to drift to the bottom and not end up in someone's pint. After a couple of weeks, the beer is said to have 'dropped bright' and is ready for serving."
—RICHARD TAYLOR,
Beer expert and host of TheBeerCast.com

KEGS

Kegs are a sleek, modern take on the cask. They are one of the most common and efficient ways of transporting and serving mass quantities of the good stuff, especially since they store their contents under pressure.

PRO: Often fresh, extremely versatile, delightfully large quantity.

CONS: Can weigh more than 150 pounds, needs to be returned to the store, requires a tap and skill to operate.

GROWLERS

If the mini keg and the bottle met through a personal ad on Craigslist and got a little freaky, the growler would be showing up at the beer bottle's house eighteen years later with a lot of awkward questions.

The growler is a big glass jug that is typically around a half gallon to a gallon. The thing that distinguishes the growler is its resealable gasket cap. More often than not, growlers are found in brewpubs and small breweries as a way to sell take-out beer.

PROS: Can be refilled at favorite brewery, fits in fridge, cool to say.

CON: Only keeps the beer fresh for about a week.

BEER BY THE GLANCE

················

KEG TYPES

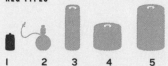

I. Mini keg (aka bubba keg):
   1.3 gallons

2. Party ball (aka disco ball):
   5 gallons

3. Home brew (aka corny keg):
   5 gallons

4. Quarter barrel (aka pony keg):
   7.75 gallons

5. Full keg (aka half barrel):
   15.5 gallons

BOTTLE TYPES

I. Pony bottle: 6–8 fluid ounces

2. Stubby: 12 fluid ounces

3. Longneck (industry standard):
   12 fluid ounces

4. Deuce deuce (rocket or bomber):
   22 fluid ounces

5. Forty: 40 fluid ounces

6. Darwin stubby: 67.6 fluid ounces

CAN TYPES

1. Squat: 8 fluid ounces

2. Standard: 12 fluid ounces

3. Sleek: 12 fluid ounces

4. Pounder, tallboy (original size): 16 fluid ounces

5. Draught flow: 16.9 fluid ounces

6. Whoop-ass, tallboy (current size): 24 fluid ounces

SHOULD I CUT MY SIX-PACK RING?

People in the biz call them "yokes." Environmentalists call them Marine Life Death Traps. But in reality, six-pack rings contribute very little to marine litter and wildlife head-locks. In fact, the manufacturer of these rings has agreed to use a recyclable plastic that will even photo-degrade within ninety days.

BOTTLES

In a lot of ways, bottles are the gold standard of beer containers. They store the beer safely, they keep beer fresh, and, most importantly, they're convenient. Beer bottles are typically made of glass, though plastic and aluminum ones do exist. They also come in a plethora of shapes and sizes and colors, and are instrumental props in many enjoyable drinking games.

PROS: Convenient, great tasting, can serve as a weapon in bar fight.
CONS: Fragile, may require opener, susceptible to the dreaded "skunking" effect.

CANS

Cans are the tube socks of beer packaging: not particularly sexy, but very effective and strangely comforting. These relative newcomers were not introduced until right after Prohibition. They proved to be cheaper, lighter, and safer than glass bottles.

PROS: Most portable, chills fast, same name as funny body parts.
CONS: Can add metallic taste to beer, doesn't make great "clink" sound when toasting.

POP A CAP:
THE GREAT DEBATE

THE CROWN
First patented in 1891 in the United States, the crown cap (aka crown cork) is the worldwide leader in capping beers. Sure, you may need an opener to pry it off. But it's this stick-to-itiveness that also makes it a more airtight enclosure.

THE TWIST-OFF
First introduced in 1966, this relative newbie bypasses the need for an opener and the danger of chipped teeth by putting the power in your hands. A simple twist and you've entered beer nirvana. Unfortunately, because the oxygen barrier is a little less impermeable, your brew might go bad sooner.

BEER BANTER

"I would kill every last man in this room for one drop of sweet beer."
—HOMER SIMPSON

BREW FACT

Early cans were conical and sealed with bottle caps to work with existing machinery. This, however, made beeramids even less stable than Lindsay Lohan.

HE WHO SMELT IT, SKUNKED IT:
SKUNKY BEER AND
HOW TO AVOID IT

Have you ever cracked open a beer on a hot summer day only to be greeted with a stinky, nostril-twitching aroma? You've just opened a skunked or light-struck beer. This occurs when ultraviolet (UV) rays strike the beer and cause certain molecules within the beer's hops to undergo a chemical change—the hops transform into sulfur compounds. Coincidentally, sulfur is the same element responsible for skunks' potent defensive smell, making the term "skunked beer" eerily accurate.

To avoid this funk, store bottles (especially clear and green bottles) out of direct light in a cool, dark place—like inside your stomach.

BEER GLASSES— not to be confused with beer goggles, which will be discussed later—are critical for two reasons. First, they hold your beer, allowing you to drink it. Second, that first reason just about says it all.

THE PINT GLASS

Holding between sixteen and eighteen ounces, the pint glass is almost cylindrical, except for a gradual widening at the top. These are a favorite of bartenders for their stackability and versatility. Bar patrons, meanwhile, like them for their stealability. The wider top makes them ideal for beers with thicker, more flavorful heads, such as stouts, porters, and ales.

PILSNER

Tall and tapered, the pilsner glass is shaped like a stretched out pint glass that holds twelve ounces. Because of its statuesque, slender build, it's perfect for showing off the body of brilliantly clear brews. The shape also helps the beer keep its head. And while it's called a pilsner glass for a reason, this accommodating glass will make any lager with a crisp body and light coloring feel right at home.

BEER BY THE GLANCE
RANDOM OTHER BEER GLASS SIZES

Pony: 5 fluid ounces
Half-pint: 8–10 fluid ounces
Schooner: 15–21 fluid ounces
Mason jar: 8–32 fluid ounces
Seidel: 16–32 fluid ounces

TULIP

The tulip glass looks similar to its floral namesake. With an almost pear-shaped body, the top crests outward, which forces a lot of the beer's volatiles up in order to make a denser head. Various pale ales— IPAs in particular—benefit from this head-boosting glass.

In addition, it may remind certain individuals to tell off-color jokes about "tulips" and "organs."

WEIZEN GLASS

The weizen glass looks like the pilsner glass's bigger, over-protective brother. Averaging about a half-liter in serving size, the weizen glass is taller and thicker than the pilsner glass and also crests outward. As with the tulip, its crested design is intended to contain a robust head while its slender build helps show off the wheat ale's body and color.

STEIN

It's no surprise that this is a product of Germany: its no-nonsense engineering makes it the ultimate drinking machine. It even makes a statement when not in use, which is why the stein is so popular among collectors. Plus, the metal lid protects your Oktoberfest lagers from bugs and errant sauerkraut particles.

BREW FACT

Beer steins wouldn't exist if it weren't for the Black Plague. The first stein was invented in Germany around 1525 and included a protective lid to prevent filthy, plague-carrying insects from entering a patron's frothy beer.

COACH SAYS

An American pint is sixteen ounces, but a British imperial pint is a full twenty ounces. Looks like there is still some Great left in Britain, after all.

FROSTED MUG

Beer purists hate that the mug's freezing temperature and the
melting ice dilute the liquid and taste. Your average American
loves it for the exact same reason. Loved or despised, this is a
classic symbol of beer hedonism—perfectly complementing
that domestic light beer and that Applebee's two-for-$20 special
after a long day at Super Target.

PLASTIC CUP

The plastic cup is similar to a pint glass, only lighter and without
the overwhelming responsibility that comes from using fragile
glassware. The smooth sides reduce head retention and the wide
mouth dissipates some of the carbonation, both of which are
important factors for improving the gulpability of cheap lager.

BEER BANTER

"I feel sorry for people who don't drink. When they
wake up in the morning, that's as good as they're
going to feel all day."
—FRANK SINATRA

THE BOOK OF BEER AWESOMENESS

NONTRADITIONAL RECEPTACLES

A seasoned beer drinker must know how to imbibe from any number of sources, preferably without soaking oneself in the process. Here are some common uncommon vessels to consider.

YARD GLASS
This three-foot-tall glass has a long widening shaft and round bulbous end. (Did that description suddenly turn erotic?) In seventeenth-century England, it was used for feasts and displays of prowess. Today, ditto. But be prepared for the rush of beer that will come when air enters the bulbous end.

GLASS BOOT
This is rumored to date back to the Prussian War when a general promised to drink from his boot if his troops won. They did. And he had a glass boot fashioned so he could still fulfill his pledge while avoiding his nasty foot funk. Slowly turn the beer boot as you reach that last bit of beer in the toe, thereby avoiding pressure buildup and the ensuing soakage.

REAL BOOT
A storied rugby tradition is to celebrate a player's first try (a goal) by shooting the boot—drinking a beer from a teammate's recently worn and muddied cleats. While nothing can make this less putrid, try pointing the toes up and toward one side to avoid having your nose buried in the business end of the boot.

FRISBEE
The ultimate symbol of carefree fun and innocence has a darker side. Despite its shallow, round shape, the average disc can hold nearly four beers. Take it slow and steady, like drinking out of your morning cereal bowl.

YARD FLAMINGO
Few things represent your social position on the sprawl of modern suburbia like an upside-down flamingo with its legs removed, beak snipped in half, and body full of beer.

Beer Chillers

ALL BEER DRINKERS have their own personal preferences when it comes to how cold they like their beer—and we respect that. But when in doubt, a beer's color is the best indicator of its optimal drinking temperature. In general, the lighter the beer's color, the colder it should be when served. An even better guideline is, the cheaper the beer, the colder it should be served. That said, there are many methods and equipment to keep your brew as frosty as need be for any occasion.

BEER BY THE GLANCE TEMPERATURE GUIDE

- Ice cold (32°F–39°F): Golden ale, ice beer, malt liquor, cheap beer
- Pretty cold (39°F–45°F): Belgian whites, duvels, hefeweizen, lager (premium/dark), pilsner
- Not that cold (45°F–54°F): Amber ale, Irish ale, lambic, porter, stout
- Cellar (54°F–57°F): Bitter, bock, brown ale, India pale ale (IPA), strong ale
- Warm (57°F–61°F): Barley wine, imperial stout

THE REFRIGERATOR
AKA FRIDGE, ICEBOX

The old faithful of beer storing apparatuses, the refrigerator is one of the best ways to chill beer. Refrigerators function as giant insulated boxes that use a heat pump to suck the heat out and keep the contents cold at an average 35–40 degrees Fahrenheit. Because of their size, these modern-day iceboxes are often considered the "home base" of beer storage and cooling.

THE KEGERATOR
AKA KEG LOCKER, WEAPON OF MASS CONSUMPTION

Perhaps one of the greatest innovations in home beer-cooling technology, the kegerator allows the user to store *and* serve draft beer straight from the keg and in the comfort of their own home. It's as if an inventor looked at a keg then looked at his refrigerator, shook his head and said, "No, no, no, this won't do at all." Once the keg is stored, it's tapped into a draft on top of the storage unit that provides a seemingly endless stream of goodness and—at its optimal 38 degrees Fahrenheit—maintains the beer's quality for months.

THE COOLER
AKA COOL BOX, PORTABLE ICE CHEST, CHILLY BIN

Portable coolers were invented in the early 1950s, and have since become a necessity in any situation that involves taking beer on the go. Initially made of metal, the cooler has since evolved into a lightweight plastic device that can keep beer cold and enjoyable for extended periods of time. While it takes a little effort to load up and cool down, the benefits are significant: cold beer always within reach and plenty of convenient, ass-friendly seating.

PROPER FRIDGE CHILLAGE TECHNIQUES

....

1. Fill her up: A full fridge is optimal for maintaining the perfect temperature throughout the opening and closing of a good party. So for the most efficient energy use, buy a lot of beer and stock it up.

2. Keep things flowing: An over-full fridge is suboptimal when it comes to cooling down your brews. Leave room for air to circulate around the precious cargo.

3. Patience is a beertue: A beertue is like a virtue, but with beer. And you will need this particular beertue to allow for the approximately ninety minutes the appliance needs to bring the beer down to a drinkable temperature.

4. Creative compartmentalization: Make sure to place some emergency beers in less obvious locations like the butter tray and vegetable crisper. This increases the odds that you can always locate some liquid, even after your guests mooch the rest.

PROPER COOLER CHILLAGE TECHNIQUES

....

1. Plan ahead: Many think that the best way to fill a cooler is to throw a bunch of ice and beer in there and close the top, but that mentality is a lot like putting ketchup on steak: just because a lot of people do it doesn't make it right.

2. Master the stack: Placing beer in a cooler isn't as simple as just dumping them in. Space management is key; you want to get as many as possible in without packing them too tightly. Be sure to leave some space between each can or bottle.

3. On thin ice: After laying down one layer of beers, pour a thin layer of ice over them. Be sure not to overdo it, as too much ice will take up precious can space.

4. Get wet: Pour a small amount of cold water over the ice and beer. Be sure not to use too much—the purpose of the water is to melt the ice slightly and make a subzero bath of water that will cool the beer in a hurry.

5. Feeling salty: The secret weapon to ensuring your brewskis get ice-cold is rock salt. It lowers the freezing point of the water and greatly magnifies your cooling ability, thereby allowing you to get warm drinks ice-cold in as little as five minutes.

COACH SAYS

Consider starting a beer cellar. Some beers truly do get better—or at least mature a little—with age. Find a room that's consistently around 50–55 degrees Fahrenheit. And make sure to put a good lock on the door.

THE KOOZIE

AKA COZY, COOSIE, HUGGER,
BEER SLEEVE, CAN COOLER,
CAN CONDOM

Like that stupid hat a mother forces on her child's head before leaving for school, the beer koozie looks ridiculous but serves a very real and very important function: keeping the beer safe from the heat. By keeping the can or bottle stored in this tight-fitting, foam rubber casing, condensation is reduced and the container has an easier time maintaining its optimal low temperature.

NO KOOZIE, NO PROBLEM.

Here are a handful of proven alternatives when a koozie is not within reach.

CROCHET
It isn't just for crazy cat ladies anymore. Thanks to the interweb, there are patterns and tutorials on how to turn a little yarn and a few friendless nights into a suds sweater for your favorite brew.

DUCT TAPE
Considered by many to be the most versatile tool ever invented, duct tape can easily be wrapped around a can or a bottle to create a koozie-like effect.

RICE KRISPIE TREATS
In a bind, the stale, uneaten Rice Krispie treats stiffening on the dessert table make a great koozie due to their dense yet malleable form.

BEER BANTER

"It was as natural as eating and, to me, as necessary. I would not have thought of eating a meal without drinking a beer."
—ERNEST HEMINGWAY

THE ALTERNATIVE CHILLING TECHNIQUES

As they say, "There's more than one way to skin a cat." However, skinning a cat seems cruel and unusual, so from now on, the saying shall be, "There's more than one way to chill a beer!" Here are a few alternative ways to keep your brew frosty.

FIRE EXTINGUISHER

For the drinker in a rush, a fire extinguisher's liquid nitrogen contents can cool a beer in a matter of seconds—as opposed to the eternal ninety minutes it takes in a fridge. Make sure it's a CO_2 extinguisher, not a chemical one, unless you like your beer dusty and toxic.

SNOWBANK

Snow is nature's icebox. Constructing a cooler out of piled snow offers a quick, all-natural method for chilling beer in a hurry. Millions of Canadians can't possibly be wrong. But remember to mark the area since many beers have been lost under snow accumulation.

TOP SHELF

Hey, it's not glamorous, but the water in a toilet tank usually runs colder than room temperature, making it a workable alternative. The circulation of cold water can reduce the temperature to a drinkable level. Plus, the displaced water in the reservoir can actually reduce your water bill. And those savings can be put toward . . . you guessed it, more beer.

CANNED AIR

Next time you need a beer chilled in an expensive and impractical way, just grab a Tupperware container big enough to hold a can, a screwdriver, and a can of compressed air. Place your beer in the container. Stab the lid with the screwdriver, being careful not to puncture the beer, insert the tube from the canned air, then blast it.

THE STORE

There is a magical place that keeps beers at the right temperature. And you don't have to do a damn thing. Just pay for it, of course.

Beer Apparel

ANYONE WHO TAKES DRINKING SERIOUSLY knows the importance of always having the right accessories. That's why we've come up with a comprehensive collection of "beer gear" to help you get your drink on.

FOAM DOME

A hat fashioned with two cup/can/bottle holders and plastic tubing leading from the open container to the wearer's mouth, the foam dome frees the drinker's hands up for other important tasks—like holding more beer.

BEER HOLSTER

Like a gun holster, the beer holster keeps a beer reliably at your side, ready to be enjoyed as soon as the one in your hand is finished, thus always preparing the busy partygoer with a steady backup.

CARGO PANTS

Depending on when you are reading this book, cargo pants are either in or out of favor with the fashion gods. But the beer gods have never wavered. Cargo pants provide a plethora of areas that some call pockets, and we call beer holders. The only downside is the TSA body scan at the end of the night to locate your house keys among the twenty-seven hiding places on your person.

BEER GOGGLES

Although not technically a physical item, beer goggles are no less real. Often unknown to the wearer, they distort one's ability to distinguish between a hottie and a nottie when approaching a potential romantic partner. Always confirm attractiveness with trusted friends (including your soda-sipping designated driver).

Beer Mixology

SOMETIMES THE BEST PIECE of beeraphernalia is simply more alcohol. While some may call it blasphemy, others believe that while beer is perfect on its own, it's even better with a little somethin'-somethin' extra.

MIXED PINTS

Mixed pints are usually concoctions that involve pouring two different types of beer into one glass to make a completely new hybrid—like a liger or a Bennifer.

BLACK AND TAN: Half-pint of ale topped with a nitrogenated stout like Guinness

HALF AND HALF: Half-pint of lager topped with stout

SNAKEBITE: Half-pint of hard cider topped with stout

SHANDIES

This refreshing concoction of beer and soda has made a sweet splash in tropical paradises around the world.

ALSTER: Beer (typically pilsner) and lemonade

RADLER: Beer and lemon-flavored soda

SHANDYGAFF: Beer and ginger ale

BOMBS

Appropriately named, these drinks involve dropping a shot of hard stuff into a pint of beer and chugging the mix down.

BOILERMAKER: A shot of whiskey or bourbon dropped into a beer

THE IRISH CAR BOMB: A mixed shot of Irish cream liqueur and Irish whiskey dropped into a pint of Irish stout

SAKE BOMB: A shot of warm sake balanced on two chopsticks over a beer, dropping when the table is pounded

PROHIBIDOS: A shot of blanco tequila dropped into a half-full pint of Mexican beer rimmed with salt

BEER COCKTAILS

Always the team player, beer can also serve as a key ingredient in a number of punches and cocktails. For the recipes below, all you need to do is mix together the ingredients, serve to your amazed friends, and look cool.

BEER MARGARITAS

12-ounce can of beer
12-ounce can of frozen limeade concentrate
12 ounces golden tequila (like Jose Cuervo Especial)
12 ounces lemon-lime soda
3 cups of ice

RUDDY MARY

12 ounces lager
2 ounces tomato juice
1 splash hot sauce

MICHELADA

6 ounces clam-flavored tomato juice (like Clamato)
2 dashes premium Worcestershire sauce
2 dashes Tabasco
2 tablespoons lime juice
1 pinch black pepper
1 pinch sea salt
12 ounces Mexican lager (like Tecate)

COACH SAYS

In Mexico, micheladas are considered a good remedy for hangovers. Behold the mighty power of clams.

Tailgating the Expert Way

There's no better reason to break out all of one's beeraphernalia than a tailgate.

TAILGATING HAS EVOLVED from a couple guys huddled around a charcoal grill, cooking dogs and downing drinks before the game, to a full-blown "event before the event," with beer being the main event of the event before the event. Without beer, there is no tailgate.

Here's what you need for improving your tailgate mastery from the pros at the National Tailgating League (theNTL.com).

BEER: This is the most important element of any tailgate. A hefty hoof to the stadium or a burnt burger will be overlooked if your guests are sufficiently inebriated, but running out of beer is an unforgivable offense.

GOOD FIELD POSITION: Location is as important in tailgating as it is in real estate. You need ample room for your setup, but you also need to be close to the event. After wolfing down tons of grub and guzzling gallons of beer, the journey to the stadium shouldn't require a map.

THEME: A themed tailgate and attention to detail are always appreciated. Everything attendees see, touch, and taste should be event-branded with team colors.

INNOVATION: Anyone can buy cool tailgating gear; diehards make their own. From keg cookers to tricked-out rides, nothing elevates your tailgating status like a one-of-a-kind invention.

TIME MANAGEMENT: Science has proven you can't throw a good party in ninety minutes. Grills should be lit and beer should be flowing hours before the actual event. Done properly, a good tailgate will provide hours of enjoyment for all involved.

POTENTIAL AUDIBLE: Mother Nature hates you. Keep a close eye on the weather and be ready for anything she may throw your way.

CHAPTER

3

BEER
DRINKING
BASICS

A wise man once said, "The gap between the lip and the glass is a mile if it is an inch."

THAT'S FORTUNE COOKIE TALK FOR, "It's really easy to spill your beer if you don't know how to drink it." Beer drinking may *seem* as easy as: bring beer to mouth, pour in, swallow, and repeat. However, a lot can go wrong in that simple process.

Without the knowledge of a full 360-degree beer-drinking procedure, an inexperienced drinker can end up with a mouthful of airy foam instead of delectable beer. But as every pro knows, there's the right way to do something, then there's the *awesome* way to do something. And beer drinking is no exception.

Grand Openings

CRACKING OPEN A BEER is much like zipping up a pair of pants: rushing through it haphazardly will lead to painful, regrettable results. With that in mind, knowing the proper way to open a beer is the first step toward enjoying it.

OPENING CANS

The act of opening a beer can has dropped down on life's difficulty list (somewhere on the "easy as" scale between falling off a log and pie). But just because it's not a complex process doesn't mean that there isn't room for awesomeness.

THE ONE-HANDER

When you just can't afford to have both hands tied up in cracking a brew, here is the simplest way to get it open.

STEP 1. Hold the can underhanded with your thumb and middle finger firmly around the rim.

STEP 2. Use your index finger to slide under the tab and open the can.

STEP 3. Use your index finger to push the tab back to its original position.

STEP 4. Enjoy the envy of your friends.

THE STEALTH OPEN

It seems like sacrilege to muffle one of the most Pavlovian reaction–inducing sounds in all of human history. But where public displays of brewskis are frowned upon, you should consider opening on the DL.

STEP 1. Get the tab in ready position, lifted but not breaking the seal.

STEP 2. Cover the top with a cotton towel or a crappy sweater.

STEP 3. Gently pull the tab and release the pressure in several short releases.

STEP 4. For the final "push" to pop through the top, create a distraction sound when you pull it, like a cough, a throat-clear, a well-placed fart, or simply say, "Psst, I'm *not* opening a beer now."

THE DIY WIDEMOUTH

Need more room for the brew to flow from can to man? Here is an easy way to convert any can into a wide-mouthed beer delivery device.

STEP 1. Open the can and place on a secure surface—a table-like object will do.

STEP 2. Place your elbow carefully over the mouth of the can.

STEP 3. Push down with medium force to expand the opening into a smile shape—being careful not to cut your elbow area on the edges.

OPENING BOTTLES

Beer needs to be securely sealed for freshness, transportation, and sometimes fermentation. However, because of this, opening a beer bottle can seem like a Herculean task if a bottle opener is unavailable—at least it would be to an amateur.

THE BLUNT-FORCE PRINCIPLE

Looking for a dramatic, cool, and possibly costly method? Well, you're in luck. This technique is similar to breaking a board with your bare hands: well-applied motion can create a substantial effect. And possibly damage furniture. Here is how.

STEP 1. Place the underside edge of the bottle cap on the edge of a hard, flat surface like a table.

STEP 2. Apply direct yet quick pressure (aka smack) the top of the cap with your palm or the side of your fist.

STEP 3. The hard edge of the surface should do the rest of the work, popping off the top.

ADVANCED VARIATION

CD TECHNIQUE

This technique is similar to opening a champagne bottle with a saber—but without the cool sword part. Align the CD with the label of the bottle. Then, with ninja-like efficiency, thrust the CD up the neck of the bottle with great speed, making sure to clip the underside of the cap. Follow through with the thrust and watch the cap take flight.

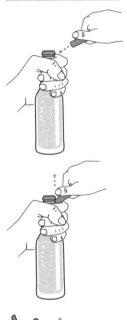

THE LEVER PRINCIPLE

This approach requires the application of a few basic physics equations to unlocking the brew. It needs an object that serves two main tasks: to break the bottle cap's grip and to provide leverage for lifting it off. Here's how to apply it using a lighter.

STEP 1. Choke up on the bottle with one hand. Insert the bottom of the lighter between your top finger and the bottom of the cap, aiming above the center of the bone between your knuckle and first finger joint.

STEP 2. Tighten your grip of the bottle. You should feel one edge of the lighter digging into the flexed muscle between your knuckles on the side of your finger. The other edge should now be pushing up on the bottle cap.

STEP 3. Push down on the metal end of the lighter. This will cause the lighter to bend the lip of the bottle cap out, away from the beer bottle. If all goes well, the cap will fly off and you will be cool.

ADVANCED VARIATIONS

BEER BOTTLE TECHNIQUE

Use the one thing that always accompanies your beer—another beer. Hold another bottle upside down and use the underside of its cap as the lever.

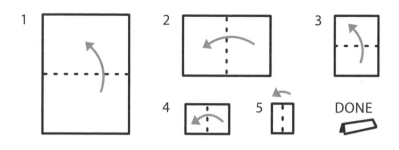

PAPER TECHNIQUE

Fold a piece of a paper as above and use the same method as with the lighter. Puts origami to shame.

TEETH TECHNIQUE

Yeth, it may be the cooleth method of all, but thith technique can altho theriouthly damage your theeth.

TAPPING KEGS

Tapping a keg is a rite of passage for any professional beer drinker. For most mortals, a keg usually represents the single largest windfall of beer. It's analogous to the slain mammoth being dragged back to the village for butchering and celebration. And it's the alpha male's (or female's) job to do it—and do it right.

HANDLE WITH CARE

Always keep a keg in an upright position. Because of the weight and size, it's nearly impossible to move a keg without angering it into a foamy frenzy. The best way to move a keg is with a dolly, or a hand truck. If a dolly is unavailable, then a steady drag (don't jerk) is a suitable alternative. The secret to dragging a keg is to place a scrap of rug, a welcome mat, or a towel under it for a smoother slide.

CHILL OUT

Once you get the keg to its final resting place, it needs some time to rest and chill out—literally. Ideally, you want to bring the brew down to 35–40 degrees Fahrenheit. Let the keg rest for one to two hours surrounded with ice. And we mean surrounded—some keg tubs only go up halfway so make sure to add a few bags of ice on top of the keg for more thorough chillage.

COACH SAYS

To minimize foam (and embarrassment), chill the tap too. The change in temperature (from cold keg to warm tap tube) produces more foam. Just place the disengaged tap on ice while the keg is chilling.

PREPARE FOR ENTRY

Make sure the tap's spigot (this is where the beer comes out) is in the off position and remove the cap from the keg's coupling (this is where you insert the tap). There are a few "slits" around the opening—these guide the notches on the tap into the correct place.

PUSH IT REAL GOOD

Lock the pump onto the keg by rotating it clockwise. Once the tap is seated properly, engage the tap by pulling the handle out, then pushing it down. Doing it quickly and decisively prevents excess pressure from escaping all over your face.

DON'T PUMP

A common mistake for most newbies is to pump as soon as the keg's been tapped. DON'T! The keg is already under pressure and any excess pumping will throw off the entire equilibrium and may lead to foamy beer the rest of the night.

COACH SAYS

Make sure you have the right tap. Domestic and imported kegs often use different tapping systems. When in doubt, get both.

THIN THE HERD

Open the spigot all the way. Always fully depress this button since partial pressure only contributes to, you guessed it, foam. Once initial flow has successfully occurred, allow about four to six cups of foam to be expunged in order to make room for better-balanced pours thereafter.

COACH SAYS

Scratches in your glass produce more foam by creating nucleation sites for the bubbles to form. If you have a glass that is scratched, rinse it with some water to coat the surface and prevent excessive bubblage.

Pouring

NOW THAT WE KNOW HOW to access the beer, we must learn to transfer it. However, getting the beer into the glass is no simple matter. Like having sex, pouring beer is a process that is more complicated than simply putting one thing into another. When poured too slowly, it can become flat and bland. When poured too quickly, it can turn into a sloppy, gross mess. Again, like sex.

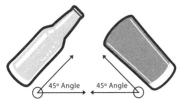

MASTER THE GEOMETRY

The most important word to remember when pouring a beer is "middle," since everything about the process is focused on balance. First, with bottle in one hand and beer glass in the other, tilt both so they are facing each other at 45-degree angles (the middle of a right angle, if you will).

AIM AND POUR, DON'T DROP

The target to aim for is the middle of the glass's side. This will give the beer a chance to hit the glass and still allow adequate space before it hits the bottom. To begin pouring, tilt the bottle toward the glass and let the beer flow from the bottle at a moderate pace.

SHIFT THE ANGLE

As the beer fills the glass and climbs up the side, space is going to begin running out. Once the beer fills to the middle of the glass, begin slowly leveling out the glass and bringing it back to a 90-degree angle.

De-foaming

AS MOST PEOPLE KNOW, some of the best baseball players get a hit only three out of every ten at bats. Like pro athletes, even the best beer drinking professional isn't perfect. Since some beers have a tendency to foam up more than others, not every pour is going to be immaculate. Because of that, excessive head can arise when it's least expected or wanted.

FACE GREASE TECHNIQUE

One of the most common—and possibly cringe-inducing—ways to dissolve excess head from a beer can be found on your face: natural oil. Simply rub a finger along a section of face (the bridge of the nose works best since this is where much of the natural facial oil collects), then swirl that finger through the beer and watch the foam retreat into thin air.

SLICE AND DICE TECHNIQUE

Another far more badass way to remove foam is with the blunt edge of a knife. As the foam crests over the top of the glass, drag the knife along the rim and scrape off the excess foam. It may look classy, but it requires you to have a knife on your person at all times. . . which is not classy.

THE BLOW TECHNIQUE

The blow is exactly what it sounds like: blowing the light, fluffy foam off of the top of the beer as if it were a dandelion. Kind of a dainty gesture, but an effective one nonetheless.

THE SCIENCE BEHIND FACE GREASE

When a beer is poured into a glass, little carbonated air bubbles rush to the top, grabbing protein molecules on their way up. The protein groups together at the top to form thick bundles of carbon dioxide, thus producing the foamy head of a beer. The foam stays on top of the beer due to the carbohydrates that are inherent in the brew.

Where does the greasy goodness of the human face come into play? Simply: oil. The natural oils of the human face reduce the surface tension of those thick carbon dioxide bubbles. This causes them to collapse and break apart, thus dissipating the excess foam at the head of the beer.

Holding Your Beer

DESPITE WHAT MOM SAYS, it's very easy to judge a book by its cover. For instance, a book with a cover featuring a ninja dinosaur playing air guitar on a pirate ship is sure to be amazing. But because people don't have book covers, we use body language to make better judgments about one another. The way a person holds their beer is no different. Here's a rundown of the most common grips.

THE EVERYMAN GRIP

Tried and true, the everyman grip is accomplished by wrapping all four fingers around the body of the bottle to meet with the thumb, keeping the bottle secure without taking any chances.

THE HANGMAN

The hangman grip involves wrapping only one or two fingers and a thumb around the neck of the bottle. Though still a very safe and reliable way to hold a beer, the hangman's lack of added finger support lets the bottle rest a little more dangerously.

THE BOOK OF BEER AWESOMENESS

THE PENDULUM

Using only the forefinger and the thumb to grip the neck of the bottle, the pendulum is a risky way to hold a beer, but damn, it looks cool. The pendulum person is a daredevil. When he sees the danger of dropping his beer bottle, he looks it in the eye, spits in its face, and sleeps with its sister.

THE TEXAS SIDE SIPPER

Lifted to the side of the mouth with two fingers, this grip looks like the drinker is taking a nip off a jug of moonshine. Few people do this naturally, so it shows that someone is wearing their Texas pride a little too much (bad) or that they just read this chapter (good).

TWO-CAN SLAM

This person holds not one, but two beers in his hand at once. This shows that someone is either good at planning ahead, or that they have a problem. Either way, they'll be fun to talk to.

AROUND THE WORLD IN FORTY CHEERS

Here is a rundown of translations and pronunciations for one of the favorite words of beer lovers around the world, "Cheers!"

LANGUAGE	WORD	PRONUNCIATION
Afrikaans	Gesondheid	Ge-sund-hate
Albanian	Gëzuar	Geh-zoo-ah
Arabic	Fisehatak	Fe-sahetek
Azerbaijani	Nuş olsun	Nush ohlsun
Bosnian	Živjeli	Zhee-vi-lee
Bulgarian	Nazdrave	Naz-dra-vey
Burmese	Aung myin par say	Au-ng my-in par say
Catalan	Salut	Sah-lut
Chamorro (Guam)	Biba	Bih-bah
Chinese (Mandarin)	Gān bēi	Gan bay
Czech	Na zdravi	Naz-drahvi
Danish	Skål	Skoal
Dutch	Proost	Prohst
Estonian	Terviseks	Ter-vih-sex
Filipino	Mabuhay	Mah-boo-hay
Finnish	Kippis	Kip-piss
French	Santé/ A la votre	Sahn-tay/ Ah la vo-tre
Galician	Salud	Saw-lood
German	Prost/ Zum wohl	Prohst/ Tsum vohl

LANGUAGE	WORD	PRONUNCIATION
Greek	Ygeia	Yamas
Hawaiian	Å'kålè ma'luna	Okole maluna
Hebrew	L'chaim	Luh-khah-yim
Icelandic	Skál	Sk-owl
Irish Gaelic	Sláinte	Slawn-cha
Italian	Salute/ Cin cin	Saw-lu-tay/ Chin chin
Japanese	Kanpai	Kan-pie
Lithuanian	I sveikatą	Ee sweh-ka-ta
Polish	Na zdrowie	Naz-droh-vee-ay
Portuguese	Saúde	Saw-oo-de
Russian	Na zdorovie/ Za Vas	Nuh zdah-rohv'-ee/ Zuh vahs
Serbian	Živeli	Zhee-ve-lee
Spanish	Salud	Sah-lud
Swedish	Skål	Skawl
Thai	Chok dee	Chok dee
Yiddish	Sei gesund	Say geh-sund

Toasting

ALL OF THIS PREPARATION comes down to this moment. The beer is so close to your innards you can practically taste it. But before you can put it to your lips, you need to pay respect to both the brew and your crew with a proper toast.

TOASTING FORMATIONS

THE CLINK AND DRINK
This classic will always get the job done. Vessels are raised, touched briefly, and brought back toward the drinkers.

COACH SAYS

When performing the physical toast, show some respect by looking the toastees in the eye at all times. Only an amateur needs to look at their beer—and you're a champion, right?

THE DOUBLE CLINK
If the Clink and Drink is like a handshake, then this is a handshake with some soul. The top rims are clinked, then bottoms of the vessels are clinked.

THE TABLE TAP

For a toast with a little more oomph, perform the basic clink, and then bring the beer down with a synchronized tap on the table, before bringing it up to the lips. This is best performed in an already loud venue.

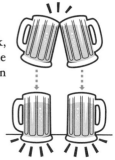

THE ON THREE

This formation is similar to a team breaking from a huddle. All vessels start off touching, and upon completion of the toast, the circle is broken by the simultaneous removal by each of the drinkers. It's a good way to rally the troops.

BREW FACT

Respect the clink. Many cultures once believed that clinking glasses would ward off evil spirits—including those devilish ones responsible for drunkenness.

BEER BANTER

"I drink to make other people interesting."
—GEORGE JEAN NATHAN

TOASTING WORDS

A toast is a sign of respect. The toaster must stand, look the other person or persons in the eye and say, well, that's where it can get tricky . . . for some people. A drinking champion knows what to do and say. Here are five approved toasts for any occasion.

1. Here's to a long life and a merry one.
   A quick death and an easy one.
   A pretty girl and an honest one.
   A drink for you—and another one!

2. My friends are the best friends.
   Loyal, willing, and able.
   Now let's get to drinking!
   All glasses off the table!

3. May your glass be ever full.
   May the roof over your head be always strong.
   And may you be in heaven half an hour before
      the devil knows you're dead.

4. Zicke, zacke, zicke, zacke, hoi, hoi, hoi!

5. Here's to your genitalia.
   May they never jail ya.

COACH SAYS

It's always a must to stand up when reciting a toast—never toast while sitting down. So please stand and read this page again.

Drinking

WE SHOULD NOT HAVE BURIED such an important point on page 71. But we weren't sure you were ready. Clearly you are now.

STEP 1. **TAKE A MAN-SIZED GULP.** Dainty sips only give you part of the experience. Get in there and taste the liquid and the head.

STEP 2. **DON'T SWALLOW YET.** Let the beer hang out with your taste buds.

STEP 3. **INHALE THROUGH YOUR NOSE.** This opens up the flavor and really brings it to life.

STEP 4. **SWALLOW.** Sorry about the delay, but we think you'll agree it was worth it.

STEP 5. **TASTE THE BEER AGAIN.** Of course. But also consider waiting for it to warm up, as lower temperatures can mask some flavor.

TASTING

There's a lot more to beer tasting than just sucking down a cold one and giving it a thumbs-up or thumbs-down. To truly judge the taste of a beer, it takes more than the words "yummy!" and "ugh!" Beer tasting is a very subtle, nuanced process that begins even before a brew touches the lips.

APPEARANCE

Before a beer is even sipped, it's judged on its appearance. Things like color, fullness, and head all play into this, as they provide telltale signs as to how the beer was made and how it will taste. Notice the color and clarity.

AROMA

The aroma of a beer can tell the taster as much about the beer as its initial appearance. The scent also contributes to the flavor of the beer, which is, of course, one of the most important aspects.

MOUTHFEEL

Once the beer is sipped, the taster then evaluates the mouthfeel, which is a judgment of the beer's texture and overall drinkability.

FLAVOR

One of the more obvious things to take into consideration is flavor. The taster judges not just the overall taste of the beer, but also other subtleties such as hoppiness, bitterness, sweetness, etc.

AFTERTASTE

Lastly, the beer is judged by the mark it leaves after it's swallowed, determining the overall finish.

TALKING LIKE A PRO

To properly judge a beer, more expressive words than "awesome" and "sucky" may be needed to accurately describe it. But who has time to finger through a dictionary? Match one word from each column to form what might pass as a coherent, well-developed opinion in the beer-tasting community!

COLUMN A	COLUMN B	COLUMN C
Warm	Colorful	Finish
Nutty	Charming	Taste
Bold	Fearless	Girth
Underwhelming	Heavy	Brew
Overpowering	Aromatic	Blend
Crisp	Bitter	Escape
Earthy	Flavorful	Treat
Unassuming	Draconian	Punishment
Tingly	Airy	Notes
Sweet	Uneven	Bouquet

THE FORBIDDEN JUICE

Sometimes a beer tastes best when enjoyed in unexpected places. Sure, a properly poured pint at a pub is a great way to end the night, but nothing starts off an adventure like a few smuggled warm brews. Be creative (and in many places criminal) and get started.

THREE WAYS TO SMUGGLE YOUR BEER ANYWHERE

Bringing your own beer is as good as free. And you feel like you stuck it to the man.

DISGUISE YOUR CAN

STEP 1: Empty a soda can—we know it tastes terrible and unbeer-like.

STEP 2: Use a can opener to remove the bottom and top.

STEP 3: Use sharp shears to cut straight up the side of the can.

STEP 4: Place over your beer and walk confidently—and straight if possible.

CREATE A FALSE BOTTOM FOR YOUR COOLER

STEP 1: Fill a cooler two-thirds full of beer.

STEP 2: Cover completely in ice.

STEP 3: Top with juice boxes and baby bottles full of formula. (Or write "organ donor" on the side).

STEP 4: Waltz past security.

KEG2-D2

STEP 1: Place a half-barrel keg on a mover's dolly cart.

STEP 2: Break an old stereo and tape electrical parts to keg.

STEP 3: Attach string to cart.

STEP 4: Pull your new "robot" around. Tell people it's your date and they'll dismiss you as a mad scientist.

FIFTY APPROVED EUPHEMISMS FOR BEER DRINKING

Being a master of the beer-drinking arts requires that one use the right jargon for the job—which is why we've provided this list of various beer-drinking euphemisms free of charge.

1. Twelve-ounce curl
2. Bending the elbow
3. Tying one on
4. Having a cold one
5. Knocking one back
6. Taking a load off
7. Guzzling
8. Sipping
9. Chugging
10. Gone drinkin'
11. Forgoing inhibitions
12. Having a nightcap
13. Indulging in libations
14. Knocking back a brew pounder
15. Going to a five o'clock meeting
16. Drowning sorrows
17. Drinking your dinner
18. Imbibing
19. Inebriating
20. Lubricating
21. Basting
22. Bellying up to the bar
23. Bottoming up
24. Black and tanning
25. Filling up
26. Sipping foam
27. Stein hoisting
28. Mug dipping
29. Pint polishing
30. Gulping
31. Going to the watering hole
32. Tapping the source
33. Going to the well
34. Hitting the trough
35. Picking your poison
36. Biting the dog that bit you
37. Celebrating life
38. Greasing the joints
39. Hitting the sauce
40. Redeeming your beer coupons
41. Loosening up
42. Widening the gyre
43. Wetting the whistle
44. Hitting the bottle
45. Overflowing the cup
46. Taking in spirits
47. Harvesting hops and barley
48. Kissing the mug
49. Having a session
50. Popping a frosty

CHAPTER

4

....

Advanced
SKILLS

The human body can do strange and amazing things.

GYMNASTICS, CALCULUS, POPPIN' AND LOCKIN': while these are all triumphs in human achievement, they pale in comparison to the advanced techniques man has developed for drinking beer.

Anyone can take beer into their mouth and swallow. But champions do more. They know that mastery of the malted monster means not just knowledge—but also artistry.

The following chapter will delve into the showmanship (and showwomanship) of beer drinking. We recommend you read (and learn) these advanced techniques with an open mind to truly understand the many ways to become a well-rounded and better beer drinker. And, dare we say, a better person.

There, we just said it.

Drinking Stances

ADVANCED STANCES

You can just sit there and sip on your bottle all night like a fragile newborn baby, or you can cowboy up, take a stand, and make a scene. Here's how.

THE LONG-DISTANCE POUR-DOWN

The long-distance pour-down is a graceful display of both gravity and precision. For extra awesome credit, attempt to bite the last drop in midair.

THE HANDS-FREE

There's a lot keeping the drinker's hands busy: throwing a horseshoe, flipping a burger, punching a hippie. This trick keeps the drinker only a head nod away from imbibing.

THE BRO

This classic stance is a purposeful lunge mixed with a bit of Napoleonic bravado. Unfortunately, the Bros Icing Bros plague of 2010 has diminished some of its shine.

Chugging

THE PRIMARY CRITERIA for a successful chug is, of course, speed. The whole point is to get the liquid from point A (the container) to point B (your insides) as quickly as possible. But a second—less discussed—criterion is efficiency. A method that results in wasted, spilled, or otherwise mishandled beer lowers the quality of a chug at any speed.

With that in mind, here are several principles one can apply to any chug.

1. **WARMER IS BETTER.**
   Ice-cold beer, while great for sitting by the dock of the bay, can cause undue difficulty during a high-speed entry. So let it mellow to just below room temperature.
2. **FLATTER IS BETTER.**
   Carbonation is what makes beer refreshing and delicious. But the hero of taste is the enemy of chug. Allow your beer to flatten a little by letting it stay opened and untouched for a few minutes.
3. **PICK YOUR TECHNIQUE BEFOREHAND.**
   There are two basic ways to chug: the trapdoor (no swallowing) and the gulp (swallowing). Our research shows that those who can trapdoor have a biological ability to relax the throat, overriding the gag reflex, so the beer can simply slide down. Everyone else must gulp. If you gulp, the best practice is to take just a few big gulps and allow your mouth to act as the reservoir between swallows.
4. **RELAX.**
   Frankie says so. And so do we. By deciding on your technique beforehand and prepping the beer to the best of your ability, you can avoid choking—and, well, choking.

CUP CHUG

This is the most basic and preferred method. Added benefit: the larger surface area of beer exposed to air allows for maximum gas release. Fewer bubbles in correlates to fewer bubbles out. Here's how to pull it off.

STEP 1. **CHOOSE THE RIGHT CUP.** This might not always be an option, but look for one that is light and easy to lift. In addition, a thinner top with a lip improves pouring quality. The simple 16-ounce plastic cup remains one of the best for the job.

STEP 2. **POUR HEADLESS.** Try to create as little head as possible and keep it at least a half inch from the rim. This allows for more control over the angle of entry.

STEP 3. **TAP IT OUT.** In the moments before chugging, tap the cup gently a few times on a hard surface to release even more of the dissolved carbon dioxide.

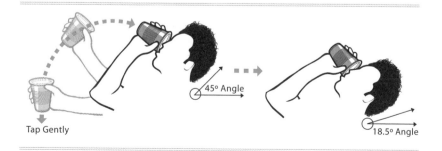

Tap Gently

45° Angle

18.5° Angle

STEP 4. **SQUEEZE IT IN.** If the cup is flexible, gently squeeze in the sides to create an oval spout out of the shorter end to improve pour control.

STEP 5. **ASSUME THE POSITION.** Tilt your head back at an approximate 45-degree angle and bring the cup to your lips.

STEP 6. **CHUG.** Take a half breath and pour the beer into your mouth. If you are trapdooring it, take your first swallow and keep it open. If you are gulping, allow the beer level in your mouth to get to a large but manageable size and swallow.

STEP 7. **TILT.** Raise the cup at a smooth but increasingly higher angle to allow all of the goodness to flow out. You will need to increase the angle of your head as well, maxing out to an optimal 18.5-degree angle, but be careful not to go too fast and lose balance—and/or your lunch.

STEP 8. **DISMOUNT.** When the cup is empty, slowly bring it and your head back to the starting position. Show the empty container if required by party law.

THE WATERFALL CHUG

This is a highly advanced cup-chug technique and should only be attempted by the most awesome drinkers.

STEP 1. Pour the contents of one can or one bottle of beer evenly among three ten-ounce plastic cups.

STEP 2. Place them in a single-file vertical line.

STEP 3. Hold the cups as shown in the illustration.

STEP 4. Lift up all three, bring the first one to your lips, and begin to chug.

STEP 5. As it empties, raise the angle of all three so the beer pours from the third cup into the second, the second into the first, and the first into your little mouth.

STEP 6. Continue until all cups are empty and you are crowned ruler of the party.

SHOTGUNNING

Shotgunning a beer is one of the most efficient ways to get a beer out of the can and into the body, and it can be done in less time than it takes to think of just the right analogy.

The name "shotgun" comes from the rapid, almost explosive force with which the beer flows out of a punctured can and into an expert drinker's mouth. While its exact origins are muddled in urban legend, its reliance on the invention of pull-top aluminum cans (patented in the Unites States in 1963) as well as its demonstration by John Cusack in the 1985 film *The Sure Thing* suggest that the technique was developed early in the second half of the twentieth century.

BREW FACT

In addition to *The Sure Thing,* shotgunning has appeared in several big-screen classics like *Dazed and Confused* and *Superbad.*

STEP 1. Hold the can horizontally with the top of the can facing away from the body. Make sure to keep the can perfectly still and straight in order to create a tiny air pocket.

STEP 2. Poke the back end of the can with a key or can opener. Once the can is punctured, push the edges of the hole inward to make the hole less sharp to prevent hand or lip lacerations.

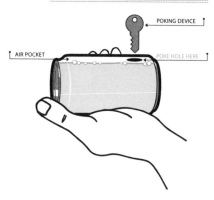

POKING DEVICE

AIR POCKET   POKE HOLE HERE

BREW FACT

An average shotgun session takes under ten seconds. However, according to the Universal Record Database, the fastest time for shotgunning a 12-ounce can of beer is 2.78 seconds.

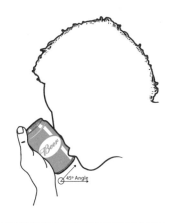

STEP 3. Close your lips around the hole, making it as airtight as possible, then bring the can up to your mouth in a diagonal position (the bottom of the can should be at a 45-degree angle to the ground).

STEP 4. Tilt the can back into a vertical position and immediately pull the trigger—pop the top. The air will rush in, forcing the beer out through the hole in the bottom and directly into the mouth in a matter of seconds.

COACH SAYS

Make sure the beer is not ice-cold when performing the shotgun—otherwise you can get some serious brain freeze.

THE BOOK OF BEER AWESOMENESS

BEER FUNNEL

Beer funneling, also known as beer bonging, is a popular drinking technique designed to let you consume a full serving (or more) of beer in a minimal amount of time.

Though the true origin of the beer funnel is unknown, it's been speculated that its design and purpose are derived from the yard of beer drinking glass. Drinking a yard of beer (see page 43) properly was a popular pub competition dating back to the 1600s. The modern beer funnel shares a similar aesthetic design and a similar purpose: speedy beer delivery.

HOW TO BUILD A BEER BONG

What you'll need:

▶ One 64-ounce plastic funnel
▶ 2–6 feet clear plastic tube
▶ Duct tape

ITEMS TO USE FOR PUNCTURING A CAN TO SHOTGUN

··················

▷ Bottle opener
▷ Key for the car you will not be driving
▷ Pen or pencil
▷ Chopstick
▷ Screw or nail
▷ Golf tee
▷ Old USB drive
▷ A sharp stick
▷ A freakishly long and sharp thumbnail

STEP 1. **ASSEMBLE DURING PURCHASE.** Before you leave the store, make sure the funnel fits snugly into the tubing. The diameter of the tube should be no more than an eighth of an inch bigger than the end of the funnel.

STEP 2. **MEASURE YOUR TUBE.** Before you cut the tubing, you need to decide if this will be a device to be used by the drinker or administered by another party. If the drinker will handle his or her own bong, then you want to keep it on the short side, around two feet, so you can easily get it over your head without too much extra slack. If someone else is going to hold it, go longer, between four and six feet.

STEP 3. **ASSEMBLE.** It does not require an advanced degree in engineering to figure this part out. Push the small end of the funnel into one end of the tubing. Make sure the connection between the tube and funnel is airtight. More importantly, make sure it is beertight too. As with most things in life, a few passes with the duct tape should suffice. Done and done.

STEP 1. **KINK THE TUBE.** With the beer funnel in hand, the first task is to "kink" the tube. To do this, place a thumb in the open end of the tube. Make sure the thumbed end of the tube is raised to the same level as the top of the funnel. Doing so should allow the tubing to hang like a U.

STEP 2. **LOAD THE BEER.** Slowly, begin pouring a beer into the funnel. Take advantage of the funnel's wide, angled sides and pour against them to prevent excess foaming. Avoid pouring the beer directly into the hose, as that will trap more air and make it more difficult to drink.

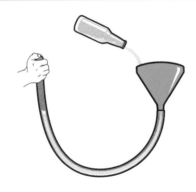

STEP 3. **SETTLE AND BURP THE BEER.** Once the beer is poured, let it settle in the tubing for several seconds; doing so allows excess air—and the subsequent foam it produces—to escape. Next, slowly release the thumb that has been blocking the open end of the tube to "burp" out more excess carbonation.

STEP 4. RELEASE THE SAUCE. With the funnel and the end of the tube still raised to the same height, place the tube in the drinker's mouth. Use the tongue to block the tube and prevent accidental flow. When ready, raise the funnel as high above the drinker's mouth as possible. This can be done in a number of ways, but the most common is for the drinker to get down on bended knee while a friend holds the funnel. Gravity is the key here; the higher the funnel is above the mouth, the faster and smoother the gulps. The average drinker can finish twelve ounces of funneled beer in two to three gulps.

STEP 5. HOIST THE MONSTER. Like Perseus holding the head of Medusa, you too must stand triumphant. Avoid swinging the bong around by the mouth-end of the tube because a broken bong will put a quick and violent end to your celebration.

BEER BANTER

"If you ever reach total enlightenment while drinking beer, I bet it makes beer shoot out your nose."
—JACK HANDEY

KEG STANDS

Few challenges in the world test a drinker's stamina like the keg stand. A staple at college parties and tailgates, keg stands are the ultimate test of mind and body. As its name suggests, a keg stand involves doing a handstand on top of the keg while continuously drinking from it. If that sounds impressive, here is how to step up to the big stand.

STEP 1. BUILD THE FOUNDATION. The most important part of a keg stand is the "stand" itself. The drinker should start by holding tightly to the grips on the top of the keg. Recruit trustworthy friends to hold the drinker's legs and hoist them up so that he'll be held between a 45- and 90-degree angle.

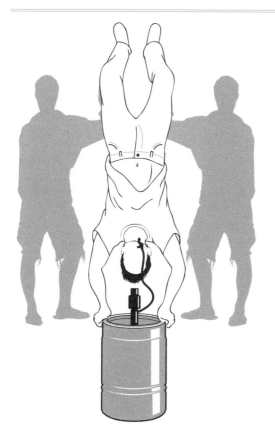

STEP 2. MAN THE TAP. Have another person place the tap into the drinker's mouth. This person will also need to man the pump.

STEP 3. DRINK IT DOWN. The beer will begin rushing into the drinker's mouth once the tap has been pressed. One of the people holding the drinker's legs should also be counting to see how long the stand lasts.

ADVANCED KEG STAND TECHNIQUES

While the standard keg stand is a great way to show off one's drinking and balancing skills, it lacks a certain flair. Here is a rundown of some stands that will keep people talking long after the party is over.

THE GARGOYLE KEG STAND

This stand is all about making a scene. It is done by perching atop the keg and balancing in a gargoyle-like pose while drinking directly from the tap. Discipline is needed to hold that pose for as long as you can, which can get quite difficult if there's a line of angry drinkers waiting for their turn at the keg.

THE GREATEST AMERICAN HERO STAND

This stand involves one person holding up their body weight with one hand while the other hand handles the beer dispensing. There are two ways to achieve this. One, be gifted with superhuman upper-body strength. This applies to a small group of gymnasts, ninjas, and Cirque du Soleil performers. Two, use the walls in a narrow hallway to walk your feet up.

THE MAGNUS

This keg stand pays tribute to the strongman competition that heats up the airwaves of ESPN13 at four in the morning. The drinker hoists the keg over his head while keeping the spigot in his mouth. If you are able to perform this technique, stay clear of remote villages whose residents might be frightened and chase you with torches and pitchforks.

Completing

WIDE RECEIVERS HAVE A TOUCHDOWN DANCE.
Wrestlers have a finishing move. Bands trash the stage. A champion beer drinker needs a victory move too. Something as monumental as drinking a beer cannot go out with a whimper.

BASIC MOVES

THE ALL-GONE
There's always one wiseass in the room who will question whether you're finishing each beer or simply pretending to polish them off to keep pace. Turning your can or cup upside down will shut his piehole once and for all.

THE SPIKE
Grab your fellow beer drinkers' attention by spiking your can onto the floor. This simple and easily executed maneuver is a sure sign that (a) you're a force to be reckoned with, and (b) you're clearly at someone else's house.

THE OVER-THE-SHOULDER FLING
Nothing says nonchalance like casually tossing an empty can over your shoulder. It's no wonder it was the go-to move for an entire generation of hard-drinking skirt chasers like Steve McQueen and Burt Reynolds.

THE SIMBA LIFT
Not only is the act of holding your empty can above your head a nice homage to *The Lion King*, but it also demonstrates the deep reverence you have for mankind's finest liquid libation.

THE POINTER SISTERS SHIMMY
Although admittedly more advanced than many of the techniques on our list, this funky full-bodied dance move does a brilliant job of letting everyone know you're excited, you just can't hide it, you're about to lose control, and you think you like it.

BELCHING: THE AUDIBLE ART

While social decorum may have many believing otherwise, belching can be a beautiful thing. A natural physiological reaction to drinking carbonated beverages, a good belch not only makes a drinker feel better physically, but it can also be turned into an art form.

As with any art, belching comes in a variety of mediums and methods. Below is a short list of better-known belches. Experiment with different methods and brews and release your inner (gastrointestinal) artist.

THE T-REX: This epic belch comes from the bottom of the gut and is shouted out with maximum volume. Not only is this formidable burp very intimidating, but it also scares weaker drinkers away from the keg or cooler.

THE ALPHABET: The belch for the learned drinker. Though the alphabet is composed of nothing more than short, simple burps that sound like each letter, it's much more difficult to pull off than it sounds. Stamina and pacing are key to popping all twenty-six letters out of the throat.

THE GRUMBLER: Best achieved with heavier beers, the Grumbler is a low, guttural burp dragged out over the longest period of time imaginable. If done right, fellow drinkers within earshot will have a hard time discerning the belcher from an angry crocodile in heat.

THE DEMON: Nothing strikes fear into others like this paranormal feat of carbonated artistry. A hybrid of the Alphabet and the Grumbler, this burp has the performer talk in a low, burped voice, making him sound like he's in need of an exorcism.

THE FOREHEAD CRUSH

With all due respect to Hulk Hogan's legendary Leg Drop, there is no finishing move quite as dramatic as the Forehead Crush. This headache-inducing maneuver lets everyone in the room know you're a no-nonsense, pedal-to-the-metal, shit-kicking alpha drinker.

STEP 1. **CHOOSE A VICTIM.** Start with an empty beer can that is devoid of any bends or dings. It's best if the can has warmed up since being emptied—room temperature is ideal. Place the can upside down and rest it on the palm.

STEP 2. **PRE-PINCH.** Slightly press the fingers into the wall of the can. This will weaken it to the point where the forehead won't need to do a painful amount of work to crush the can.

STEP 3. **SEAL THE DEAL.** When it's time to get the job done, fling the can toward the forehead, continuing to crush the fingers into the walls of the can. When the can meets forehead, let the hand do all the work to reduce the pain and increase the impact. If the can has been gripped right, it should crumple into a tiny metal pancake as it hits. If not, use some cooler ice to treat the swollen forehead area.

THE KEG TOSS

Just because the keg is tapped doesn't mean the fun is over. The keg toss keeps the party going and testosterone flowing.

FOR HEIGHT
To emulate your favorite strongman competition, use the pendulum method. From the pre-NBA free-throw stance, use a fluid (no pun intended) swinging motion with the keg between your legs to generate some momentum. Release backward over your head at the apex of your swing.

FOR DISTANCE
This is an ode to Thor. Like throwing a mighty hammer, discus, or little person, the key is centrifugal force. Hold the top of the keg with both hands and begin moving your whole body in a circular spin movement. Increase the speed, picking up momentum and extreme dizziness until you release the keg in the general direction you want.

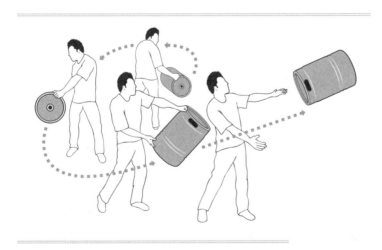

Beer Tricks

BEER MAKES EVERYTHING MORE FUN, after all. But aside from sports debates and interesting stories from that one crazy night in Tijuana, most people have little to offer in terms of entertainment while having a few pops. Enter beer tricks: a set of specifically designed techniques that will help you amaze and astound everyone with your mastery of beer's magical powers.

THE INSTANT FREEZING BEER

The Instant Freezing Beer is an eye-grabbing trick that can be done very easily while giving fellow drinkers the idea that the performer is actually a witch in need of a burning.

THE EFFECT: You show a clear glass bottle of beer. You open it up and pour out a little bit. Then you tap the bottle on the table and it immediately begins to freeze—right before their very eyes.

THE SECRET: The beer has already been chilled in the freezer just to brink of freezing—but not over. Put an unopened bottle in the freezer for about three hours. After it's close to frozen but still liquid, place in the refrigerator just before you want to bust it out.

THE PERFORMANCE: When it's time to perform, crack open the bottle. Gently pour some beer out and make a loud throat-clearing noise. With the audience's attention captured, tap the top of the bottle hard with the bottom of another bottle. This will cause the beer to release carbon dioxide. With the carbon-dioxide molecules released, the beer will begin forming

MAGIC TRICK VS. BEER TRICK

••••••••••••••••

Done in a cloud of dry ice	vs.	Done in a bar
Performed to get friends	vs.	Performed for friends
Impresses kids	vs.	Impresses potential mates
Magic word: abracadabra	vs.	Magic word: [never use one]

ice crystals. Act as if it is possessed, throw it against a wall, and run away (optional).

THE AMAZING SPIDER-BOTTLE

A crowded party can often present drinkers with a problem: where to place empties. Thanks to this adhesive illusion, a savvy drinker can get rid of an empty while making an impression.

THE EFFECT: You finish your beer and rub the bottle up and down the wall in the corner of a room—and amazingly, when you let go, it stays stuck to the wall.

THE SECRET: Friction can heat up the paint on the walls, making them sticky enough to hold the empty bottle in place.

THE PERFORMANCE: Scout the right location. Look for a corner in which both sides are painted. Next, make sure the bottle is dry—wipe off any condensation. Place the bottle firmly in the corner with the glass making contact with both of the corner's walls. Quickly rub the bottle up and down against the walls a few times. Carefully let go and the bottle should stay up. *Note:* This trick can ruin the paint job on the walls, so only perform it in the home of someone you don't really care for.

THE IMPOSSIBLE BLOW

Few tricks are easier to perform and more embarrassing for an unsuspecting friend. It can also work as a beer bet to earn you free drinks.

THE EFFECT: You turn an empty bottle on its side and place a bent bottle cap just barely inside the neck. Then you challenge a friend or random townie to blow the cap into the bottle.

THE SECRET: The force of the air will reflect from inside the bottle and bounce back out, keeping the cap from entering the bottle. Try as they might, it just won't happen.

THE PERFORMANCE: You just need to leave about a quarter of the bent cap sticking out. As your friend tries mightily to blow it in, be sure to feign surprise when it just doesn't go in.

IN CASE OF BAR FIGHT, DON'T BREAK GLASS

....

Hold on to your seats: movies aren't 100 percent accurate. Do you remember when the loose-cannon main character smashes a bottle on the bar to create a weapon he then waves, saying, "Who wants a piece of this?" That's not a real bottle. Scored sugar glass is used since real glass is too unpredictable. As an amorphous solid, it can crack in any old direction.

Bring on the Games

DRINKING GAME BASICS

....

DRINK:
The term "drink" refers to the amount of beer a player consumes as a penalty (or reward). A drink is typically one to two ounces of beer or about a two-second sip.

SOCIAL:
The point in a game where all the players must take a drink together.

HOUSE RULES:
These are the idiosyncratic laws developed by a group. These supersede all other rules, even those in this book. Always make sure you are familiar with any house rules before you partake.

SUDSMANSHIP:
This is the drinking version of sportsmanship. Sore losers and sorer winners can ruin a party in the same amount of time it takes to shotgun a beer. Play with honor or don't play at all.

NOW THAT YOU'RE thoroughly soaked with some proper beer wisdom, it's high time you upgrade to champion status. Because a true mastery of beer must also include a working knowledge of beer-related games.

Far from a new phenomenon, drinking games are nearly as old as alcohol itself. The earliest known reference to these booze-fueled contests can be traced back to 385 B.C.E. in Plato's *Symposium*. This ancient document carefully lays out the rules to Kottabos, a game of skill in which drops of wine were flicked from a player's cup at a metal disk several feet away. Winners were rewarded for their accuracy with special cakes and kisses from serving boys (it was Greece, after all).

Kottabos, and other games like it, continued to develop over the years and now there are literally thousands of games for the discriminating imbiber to choose from. Lucky for us all, we've carefully tested, selected, and broken down the best beer drinking games and put them into words that will be just as easy to understand after your first or your umpteenth beer. And to help you navigate which game is best suited for your beer drinking desires, we've also included this handy decision chart.

Let's play!

WHAT SHOULD I PLAY?

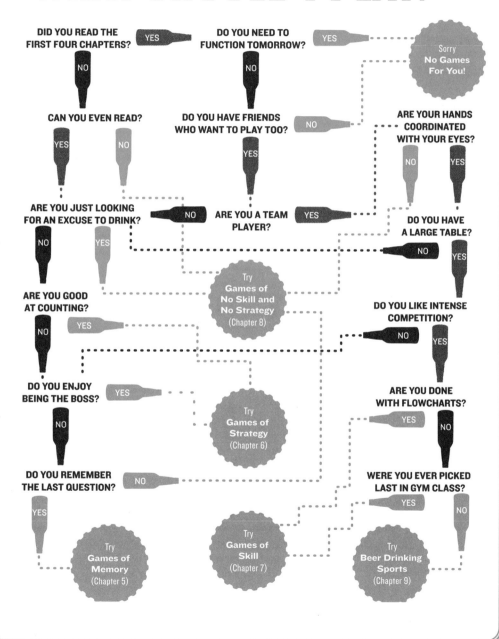

DID YOU READ THE FIRST FOUR CHAPTERS? YES

NO

DO YOU NEED TO FUNCTION TOMORROW? YES

NO

Sorry **No Games For You!**

CAN YOU EVEN READ?

YES   NO

DO YOU HAVE FRIENDS WHO WANT TO PLAY TOO? NO

YES

ARE YOUR HANDS COORDINATED WITH YOUR EYES?

NO   YES

ARE YOU JUST LOOKING FOR AN EXCUSE TO DRINK? NO

NO   YES

ARE YOU A TEAM PLAYER? YES

DO YOU HAVE A LARGE TABLE?

NO   YES

ARE YOU GOOD AT COUNTING?

NO   YES

Try **Games of No Skill and No Strategy** (Chapter 8)

DO YOU LIKE INTENSE COMPETITION?

NO   YES

DO YOU ENJOY BEING THE BOSS? YES

NO

Try **Games of Strategy** (Chapter 6)

ARE YOU DONE WITH FLOWCHARTS?

YES   NO

DO YOU REMEMBER THE LAST QUESTION? NO

YES

WERE YOU EVER PICKED LAST IN GYM CLASS?

YES   NO

Try **Games of Memory** (Chapter 5)

Try **Games of Skill** (Chapter 7)

Try **Beer Drinking Sports** (Chapter 9)

CHAPTER

5

GAMES
— of —
MEMORY

Thinking meets drinking.

WHEN TRUE COMPETITORS GET TOGETHER and discuss the greatest head-to-head duels of all time, they generally mention Ali vs. Frazier, Hulk Hogan vs. Andre the Giant, or Biggie vs. Tupac. But those all pale in comparison to the greatest head-to-(beer)head battle that occurs each time you crack open a beer: drinking vs. thinking.

In one corner you have your brain, a highly evolved organ designed to help you learn, retain, and retrieve previously presented material. And in the other you have beer, a tasty liquid so powerful it can make you forget your name, the date, and the fact that you totally suck at singing karaoke. Put them together and what do you get? The basis for a full lineup of tantalizing games!

Buffalo Club

AKA BUFFALO,
WELCOME TO THE CLUB

WHAT YOU'LL NEED
BESIDES BEER

> An ability to remember one
very simple rule

Man is a social animal who has always felt an innate need to align himself with those who share his interests and core values. This deep-rooted desire to connect with like-minded souls can be traced back to prehistoric times, when he would hunt in packs. And this tribal connection is alive and well (not to mention well-refreshed) today with the Buffalo Club.

SETUP

> Buffalo Club is played with as many players as you want.
> All players must have a beer in their possession.
> Before the game can begin, a new player must be enrolled in the Buffalo Club by an initiated member.
> The new player must interlock their lefty pinky around the left pinky of the initiated member and repeat the following phrase: "I (state your first and last name) promise to follow all the rules of the Buffalo Club."

GAME PLAY

> Once initiated, Buffalo Club must be played for the rest of your life. The rules are valid anywhere, anytime, and with any kind of alcoholic beverage (yes, even appletinis).
> All initiated players must hold and drink beer in their non-dominant hand at all times.

SCORING (DRINKING) METHOD

▷ If somebody yells "Buffalo Club!" out loud when you are holding a beer in your dominant hand, you must drink the rest of the beer you're holding.

▷ If you accidently drink it with your dominant hand when "Buffalo Club!" is called, you must drink an additional drink.

▷ If you call "Buffalo Club!" on somebody when he is actually holding the beer with the proper hand, he may call "False Buffalo!" and you are obligated to finish your own beer.

COACH SAYS

Special care must be made when drinking with left-handed Buffalos.

Fuzzy Duck

WHAT YOU'LL NEED BESIDES BEER

❱ A loose and limber tongue

There's nothing funnier than watching a prudish player scream out a stream of obscenities. That's the appeal of Fuzzy Duck, a tongue-twisting, mouth-mangling, profanity-inducing game that challenges players to correctly repeat a simple phrase. Sound easy? It's ducking not!

SETUP

▷ Fuzzy Duck is played with a minimum of four players.

▷ Players must sit in a circle with their beer within arm's reach.

GAME PLAY

▷ One player begins by saying "Fuzzy duck" and passes play to the left.

▷ The next player must answer "Ducky fuzz," which continues to pass play to the left.

▷ Players alternate the phrases "Fuzzy duck" and "Ducky fuzz" in order.

BREW FACT

Tongue twisters exist in nearly every language, including American Sign Language.

- Any player may also say "Does she?" and this phrase changes the order to the opposite direction and the passing word to "Fuzzy duck."
- Play continues quickly until someone invariably messes up (it will happen sooner than you think).

SCORING (DRINKING) METHOD

- If a player gets tongue-twisted she receives one point and must take a drink.
- Any player who misses her turn receives one point and must take a drink.
- If a player speaks out of turn she receives one point and must take a drink.
- A player is eliminated once she accumulates three points.
- Play continues until there is only one player remaining.

HOW TO DECIDE WHO GOES FIRST

················

Sure, flipping a coin or playing rock-paper-scissors are fine ways to determine playing order, but sometimes you need to make a change and crank it up a notch.

- ❯ Biggest or smallest earlobes
- ❯ Most tattoos
- ❯ Most piercings
- ❯ Dance-off
- ❯ Longest last name
- ❯ First person to drop a deuce on command
- ❯ Most push-ups
- ❯ Least money in wallet
- ❯ Shortest pinkie
- ❯ Stare-off
- ❯ Closest birthday to today
- ❯ Worst smelling shoes
- ❯ Worst smelling

COACH SAYS

Fuzzy Duck is a game of real strategy. Look at the wrong player when you utter your phrase to try and trick them into thinking it's his turn.

I Never

WHAT YOU'LL NEED BESIDES BEER

················

❯ A group of uninhibited perverts

If you've never played I Never, you're in for a very pleasant surprise. A variation of Truth or Dare, this hilariously risqué game helps loosen the tension in a crowd by revealing a group's deepest, darkest secrets. As an added bonus, it's the perfect game for determining carnal compatibility with your fellow players.

COACH SAYS

Stay away from the one who took a sip when someone said, "I never made a sex tape with an alpaca." Trust me.

SETUP

▷ I Never requires a minimum of three players—but more players equals more fun.

▷ Lurkers are not recommended—everyone must be involved to encourage optimal rule compliance.

▷ Players sit in a circle with their beers within arm's reach and hold up all ten of their fingers (sorry, Telly Savalas).

GAME PLAY

▷ Players take turns making a statement beginning with the phrase, "I never . . ."

▷ Play continues in a clockwise formation.

SCORING (DRINKING) METHOD

▷ Any player who cannot agree with a statement must take a sip of his drink and put down one finger. For example, if someone says, "I never played this game before," then any player who has played before must drink and put down a finger.

▷ If no one drinks to the statement, then the player who made the statement must drink and put down one finger.

▷ The player who makes the statement must also drink and put down one finger if he cannot agree with his own statement. This is referred to as a "self-sacrifice" and is often used to trick another player into admitting something quite revealing.

▷ A player is eliminated once he has all ten fingers down.

▷ Play continues until only one player remains.

▷ No explanation or elaboration is required about one's response.

I NEVER QUESTION SUGGESTIONS

················

Getting other players to admit to outrageous stuff is what makes this game so much fun, so be creative with your statements. Here are some sample questions to take for a test drive before you think of your own:

❯ I never peed in a public pool.
❯ I never toked up with my English teacher.
❯ I never slept with my boss.
❯ I never cheated on a test.
❯ I never got aroused by Betty or Veronica.
❯ I never fooled around in my parents' bed.
❯ I never had cosmetic surgery.
❯ I never cheated on my taxes.
❯ I never fantasized about someone else during sex.
❯ I never faked an orgasm.
❯ I never lied to get a job.
❯ I never had a one-night stand.
❯ I never used a fake ID.
❯ I never paid for sex.
❯ I never laughed so hard I peed.
❯ I never ate my own booger.
❯ I never talked my way out of a traffic ticket.
❯ I never went a full day without wearing clothes.
❯ I never cross-dressed.

Name Game

WHAT YOU'LL NEED BESIDES BEER

••••••••••••••

❯ A rudimentary understanding of the alphabet

There are more than 200,000 people living in Hollywood and every one of them has a name. Some of them are alliterative (Sharon Stone), some of them are grandiose (Engelbert Humperdinck) and some of them are downright crude (Terra Hymen). The one thing they share in common is that they can all be used in the Name Game, a fabulous drinking contest that challenges players to rattle off the names of the rich and famous. It looks like all of those years of reading *People* magazine in your dentist's office have finally paid off!

SETUP

◗ The Name Game is played with a minimum of two players.
◗ Players sit in a circle with their beer within arm's reach.

GAME PLAY

◗ One player begins by saying the first and last name of a famous person. For example, let's begin with American statesman and brewer Samuel Adams.
◗ Play passes to the next player who has to say the name of a famous person whose first name starts with the first letter of the last name of the previous famous person. For example, Angelina Jolie, because Adams and Angelina both begin with the letter "A."
◗ Play continues around the circle in a clockwise formation.
◗ If a player comes up with a name that has double initials (e.g., Jesse James) the direction gets reversed.
◗ Play continues quickly until someone invariably messes up.

SCORING (DRINKING) METHOD

▷ If a player takes longer than three seconds to come up with a name, she receives one point and must take a drink.

▷ If a player uses the wrong initial to start the name, she receives one point and must take a drink.

▷ If a player repeats a name that has already been used, she receives one point and must take a drink.

▷ If a player makes up a name (e.g., Dick Stroker) or uses a nickname (e.g., Iron Mike instead of Mike Tyson) or uses a fictional character's name (e.g., Holden Caulfield), she receives one point and must take a drink. Names must be real people, dead or alive.

▷ If a player utters the name of a one-word celebrity (e.g., Cher, Prince, or Snooki), the next person in the circle misses her turn.

▷ If a player uses a triple-word name (e.g., Sarah Jessica Parker), everyone must take a drink.

▷ After a triple-word name, play begins again with the next player saying a brand-new name.

▷ A player is eliminated when she accumulates three points.

▷ Play continues until only one player remains.

ALTERNATE RULE

••••••••••••••

Add some difficulty by starting each round with a particular category: actors, athletes, porn stars, etc. This adds another layer of thinking to your drinking.

BREW FACT

The longest name in history is: Adolph Blaine Charles David Earl Frederick Gerald Hubert Irvin John Kenneth Loyd Martin Nero Oliver Paul Quincy Randolph Sherman Thomas Uncas Victor William Xerxes Yancy Zeus Wolfeschlegelsteinhausenber-dorft Sr. (Mr. Hubert Wolfe for short).

Rhymes

WHAT YOU'LL NEED BESIDES BEER

··············

❱ An appreciation for Dr. Seuss

You don't need a rhyme or reason
to play the game of Rhymes,
You simply need a little beer
and friends who like good times.
So go gather in a circle
and let this game begin,
When there's this much beer involved
everybody will win.

SETUP

▷ Rhymes is played with a minimum of two players.
▷ Players sit or stand in a circle with their beer within arm's reach.

COACH SAYS

Keep this game fun and simple with words like "ale" and "beer" because no one likes a wiseass who tries to drop in words like "difficult" or "orange."

BREW FACT

There are no perfect rhymes for the word "month." If someone says it, challenge it!

GAME PLAY

▷ The first player says a word, any word.
▷ The next player must say a new word that rhymes with the previous word.
▷ Play continues in a clockwise formation until someone messes up.

SCORING (DRINKING) METHOD

▷ If a player takes longer than three seconds to come up with a word, he receives one point and must take a drink.
▷ If a player says a non-rhyming word, he receives one point and must take a drink.
▷ If a player repeats a word, he receives one point and must take a drink.
▷ If the first player picks a word that doesn't seem to have a rhyme, the next player can challenge him to come up with a rhyme for his own word. If they can't, he takes a drink and receives one point. If he can, the challenger must drink twice and receives two points.
▷ Play begins again with the next player saying a brand-new word. In this case, the word does not have to rhyme with the previous word.
▷ A player is eliminated once he has accumulated three points.
▷ Play continues until only one player remains.

FIFTEEN WORDS WITH UNUSUAL PERFECT RHYMES

··············

Keep these zingers in your back pocket to rule the next game of Rhymes.

ARUGULA rhymes with *BUGULA*
  (a type of fern)
CHAOS rhymes with *NAOS*
  (a chamber in Greek temples)
CIRCLE rhymes with *HURKLE*
  (to pull in all your limbs)
ELSE rhymes with *WELS*
  (a kind of fish)
MIDST rhymes with *DIDST*
  (a form of the word "did")
MUSIC rhymes with *AGEUSIC*
  (to lack a sense of taste)
ORANGE rhymes with *BLORENGE*
  (a hill in Wales)
PINT rhymes with *RYNT*
  (a word farmers use to get a cow to move)
PURPLE rhymes with *CURPLE*
  (the hindquarters of a horse)
RHYTHM rhymes with *SMITHAM*
  (fine malt dust)
SILVER rhymes with *CHILVER*
  (a female lamb)
TOILET rhymes with *OILLET*
  (an eyelet)
WASP rhymes with *KNOSP*
  (a decorative knob)
WIDTH rhymes with *SIDTH*
  (another word for "length")
WOMAN rhymes with *TOMAN*
  (a Persian coin)

Thumper!

WHAT YOU'LL NEED BESIDES BEER

> One sturdy table

Anyone who likes to get a little rowdy (who doesn't?) when they drink is sure to love Thumper! This awesomely raucous game encourages players to pound on a tabletop while they take turns flashing hand signs like drunken Vikings with West Coast gang affiliations.

SETUP

▷ Thumper! is played with a minimum of five players.
▷ Players sit at a table with their beers within arm's reach.
▷ Each player picks a unique hand gesture (okay sign, thumbs-up, hang ten, etc.).
▷ Each player should take a few moments to familiarize everyone with his or her gesture.

GAME PLAY

▷ All players pound the table in unison like they're playing the drums.
▷ The first player yells out, "What's the name of the game?" and all the players scream, "THUMPER!" The first player then responds, "And why do we play it?" All the other players scream a variation of "To get fired up!" (Or any other F word that comes to mind.)
▷ The first player does a hand gesture for a beat and then immediately follows it with another player's gesture. This is called a "pass."
▷ The player whose gesture was just introduced must now perform her own gesture for a few beats and immediately follows it with another player's gesture.

SCORING (DRINKING) METHOD

▷ Any player who misses her pass receives one point and must take a drink.

▷ Any player who messes up another player's gesture receives one point and must take a drink.

▷ Any player who performs a motion that no one recognizes receives two points and must take a drink.

▷ After each drink, everyone starts thumping the table again and the player who performed the pass begins again by yelling out, "What's the name of the game?"

▷ A player is eliminated once she has accumulated five points.

ADVANCED HAND GESTURES

Sure, a peace sign, the middle finger, and the jerk-off gesture are all acceptable, but here are eight more examples you can bring to the Thumper table.

TUNE IN TOKYO
This gesture is made by twisting your nipples.

BUMPIN' UGLIES
This gesture is made by poking one index finger through the hole formed by your other index finger and thumb.

CUT IT OUT
Uncle Joey's signature movement from *Full House*.

2 LEGIT 2 QUIT
The eponymous move from M.C. Hammer's chart-topping, shark-jumping song.

AIR QUOTES
This gesture is made by raising both hands to eye level and pumping the index and middle fingers.

THROAT SLASH
Run your "thumbs-up" rapidly across your throat to make the classic "I *keeel* you" sign.

THE SHOCKER
Curling your ring finger and thumb down while extending your remaining fingers makes a gesture that's just too explicit for this family-friendly book.

JAZZ HANDS
Wave both hands, palms out, with your fingers splayed to create the international sign for fabulousness.

GAMES

— *of* —

STRATEGY

Time for blood, sweat, and beers.

UNLIKE OTHER GAMES that focus on the warm embrace of camaraderie or the fickle finger of fate, games of strategy are about premeditated victory. They play into our deeply ingrained human need to dominate, manipulate, and make others fetch the beer.

This aggressive, deceptive side of our nature may not be the noblest part of humanity. But it needs some exercising. Success in life is largely dependent on how you analyze your competition, take advantage of opportunities, and lead others. In short, you need a manipulative side, even if you don't particularly like it.

So how do we reconcile this inner conflict? Well, with these games of strategy, of course.

Asshole

Arguably the best known of all strategic drinking games, Asshole requires mental dexterity and a degree of cunning. It also relies on our innate need to both subjugate and displace our peers in even the most ramshackle hierarchy. Have *Lord of the Flies* and the good seasons of *Survivor* taught us nothing? No? Well, Asshole will.

WHAT YOU'LL NEED BESIDES BEER

....

> A deck of playing cards

SETUP

- ▷ Asshole is ideally played with four or more players. If more than six are playing, you may want to use two decks.
- ▷ Before the game starts, players agree to card rankings. Typically, cards are ranked lowest to highest (four is the lowest and ace is the highest). Twos are clear cards that automatically clear the round and trump anything and everything played; threes are wild cards and the player may choose any value except two.
- ▷ All of the cards are dealt out evenly among the players, facedown.
- ▷ All players look at their own hand but don't show it to the others.

COACH SAYS

In all games involving cards, always deal starting with the player to the left, continuing in a clockwise direction. Don't question it, that's just the way it is.

GAME PLAY

▷ The player who has the four of clubs starts by laying down that card and play begins clockwise.

▷ Players, in order, must discard a card higher than the previous card or pass on that turn. For example, when a four is the lead card, the next player must play a card equal to or higher than a four, then the next player has to play equal to or higher than that. Suit does not matter.

▷ If a player lays down a card equal to the one on the table (e.g., playing a four on a four), the next player in line is skipped.

▷ A player may throw out any card to start a round. Multiples of the same card can also be used to start a round. For example, if the player has two fours, this person may play both cards. The next player must play two (not one and not three) cards of the same value equal to or higher than four (e.g., the other two fours, two fives, or two of anything higher).

▷ A new hand starts when someone plays a two (the clear card) or all players pass. The last player to play a card leads the next hand.

▷ Play continues until all players get rid of their cards. The first player out of cards is the President for the next round, the next player out becomes the VP, the player out after that is Secretary, and the last person out is the Asshole.

▷ As a penalty, the Asshole must always deal and clear the cards for all the remaining games. He must also give the two best cards in his hand to the President while the President gives his two worst cards to the Asshole in exchange.

- The President is the first player to start each round and play continues in order down the ranks.
- At the end of each round, players move seats in order to reflect their rank and proper playing order based on who finished first. Rank may change after each round and seats must be adjusted accordingly.
- When dealing, the Asshole must always start with himself and distribute the cards in order of rank from low to high.

SCORING (DRINKING) METHOD

- If you are skipped or have to pass on your turn, you must take a drink.
- When three cards of the same value are played in one round (three in a row or triples), it's a "social" and everyone drinks.
- The President can make any player drink at any time; nobody can make the President drink.
- The VP can make any player drink at any time except the President and only the President can make the VP drink. The Secretary can make any player drink at any time except the President and VP and only the President and VP can make the Secretary drink.
- The remaining players can only make the Asshole drink. The Asshole cannot make any other player drink and must refill any other player's beer when asked; however, he must first have the President's permission to do so.
- If the President remains President for three consecutive rounds he must initiate a "board meeting," which starts with a "waterfall" (everyone drinks and is not allowed to stop drinking until the rank above them stops drinking) and ends with the President issuing a special edict—a random yet mandatory rule that is selected for all remaining games (see page 116 for examples of other rules).

Ten Advanced Presidential Edicts

DESIGNATED DRINKER: After winning three games, the President can assign a "designated drinker" to do his penalty drinking.

THE COUP: If an Asshole wins a game and is elevated to President, she has the right to call a vote among other players to decide if the previous President should be automatically crowned the new Asshole.

LAST CARD RULE: If a player gets down to one card without announcing it, he must drink. The President determines how much that player drinks.

COMMUNISM: Each player, no matter his title, turns to the player to the right and lets him blindly select a card.

SURVIVOR: Once titles are assigned, the Asshole is voted off. Keep playing until the last man is standing.

LOBBYIST GROUPS: Each player without a title takes up a cause to lobby (such as socials, waterfalls, etc.), and when she is down to her last card, she makes everyone participate in her cause.

GREEN CARDS: If a new player wants to join the game, the President and other players devise a drinking-based "citizenship test" he must pass in order to play.

ROLE REVERSAL: Place a joker in the deck. When the joker is played, all roles are swapped. The President becomes the Asshole, the Asshole becomes the President, and so on down the line.

MR. THUMB: The President places her thumb on the table; the last person to follow suit must drink.

LITTLE MAN: Before taking a drink, all players must pretend to pick up a "little man" from the lip of his cup, and replace him after drinking. Forget, and you must drink more.

B-E-E-R

Drinking, bluffing, spelling; B-E-E-R has it all! A fast-paced game, B-E-E-R tests its players' ability to match cards. While many other games in this world like to dress themselves up with clever, academic-sounding names like Jeopardy, Pictionary, and Grab Ass, B-E-E-R is a game that knows what it is, knows what it's used for, and rewards its players accordingly.

WHAT YOU'LL NEED BESIDES BEER

....

❱ Two decks of playing cards

SETUP

▷ B-E-E-R is best played with three to five players.

▷ Players arrange themselves around a table.

▷ Four cards are dealt out to each player, facedown.

▷ All players look at their own hand but don't show it to the others.

▷ A set amount of cups filled with two ounces of beer are placed in the center of the table totaling one less than the number of players playing. For example, if there are four players, three cups are needed.

GAME PLAY

▷ Each player's goal is to make her four cards into a set of four of a kind by drawing new cards and discarding unwanted ones.

▷ No player may have more than five cards or fewer than four cards at any given moment. Players must hold their cards in their hands.

▷ Play begins when the first player selects the top card from the remaining deck and then discards one card to the right, facedown on the table.

▷ The next player picks up the discarded card, discards a card to her right, and play continues with the next player.

- The last player discards her card into a discard pile, while the first player continues to select cards from the original pile.
- Players are not allowed to pick up a discarded card until they have discarded one, so if they are slow, their piles could build up.
- As soon as any player has a set of four cards of the same value, she is allowed to take a beer from the middle of the table.
- As soon as any player grabs a beer, all the other players must also grab a beer.

SCORING (DRINKING) METHOD

- The player who ends the round without a beer gets the letter B and must drink one of the cups from another player and refill it. A player losing a round for the first time earns the letter B, then at the next loss the letter E, and so on until spelling out B-E-E-R.
- Beers can be reached for at any time so long as the beer is not actually touched. This is called bluffing and causes someone to improperly grab a beer prematurely.
- If a player grabs a beer prematurely, she automatically gets a letter and must take a drink.
- In some cases, a player may get four of a kind and grab a beer without the other players noticing. If enough time passes, the player who grabbed the beer may yell "social" and the players who didn't realize there were beers missing automatically get a letter and must take a drink.
- When a player has accumulated all four letters in B-E-E-R, she is eliminated from the game and must drink from all the remaining cups and refill them all except one. At that time, the number of cups used in the game is reduced by one.
- The game continues until only one person remains. That person is declared the winner.

Beeramid

This game is like a country song in a nutshell. It is full of lying, cheating, beer drinking, and card playing. The only missing element is a fiddle solo. But do not focus on the lack of the redneck violin; enjoy the unabashed opportunity to lie through your teeth. And through any orifice of your choosing.

WHAT YOU'LL NEED BESIDES BEER

••••••••••••••••

❯   A deck of playing cards

SETUP

▷ Beeramid requires at least three players but it gets more interesting with more players—up to eight.

▷ A dealer sets up a pyramid of cards facedown on a table: five cards on the bottom row; four on the next; then three, two, and one on the top. (See illustration on next page if you're confused.)

▷ Each player is dealt four facedown cards. Players are allowed to look at their cards but must not let any of the other players see them.

GAME PLAY

▷ Play begins when the most bottom left card of the pyramid is flipped faceup by the dealer.

Once you get the hang of basic Beeramid, try playing with two decks. There will be two of each card, making the bluffing way more interesting.

DRINKER DICTIONARY
BEERAMID

....

Do confuse this game with an actual beeramid.

n. An improvised sculpture created solely out of empty beer cans— often as a way to celebrate the number of cans consumed.

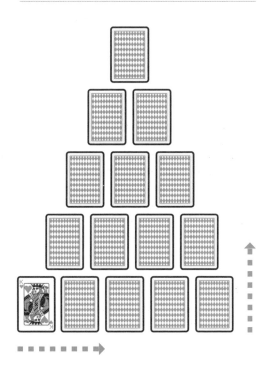

SCORING (DRINKING) METHOD

▷ Any player holding a card matching the same value (number) of the turned card may give out a drink. If they have more than one matching card, they are allowed to give out additional drinks for each match they possess.

▷ Players may also bluff and pretend to have a match.

▷ When another player is told to drink, he can either accept the drink or call the bluff.

▷ If the player was bluffing and his bluff is called, he must drink double.

▷ If the player was not bluffing, he must quickly show his card to prove it and the player that mistakenly called the bluff must now drink double.

▷ After each round, the original card is flipped facedown and the next card in the row is flipped faceup. Play continues down the row.

▷ After the final card in each row is flipped, play continues up to the next row starting from the left. Play continues until the very top card is flipped.

▷ Each card represents one drink and each row represents the number of drinks. Each card in the bottom row is worth one drink, then two drinks for the cards in the next row, then three, four, and five drinks for the following rows.

▷ Drinks can be given out in any combination, all to one player or to several players.

▷ Whichever player(s) have a match to the last card, without bluffing, win.

▷ If no one has a match for the last card, everyone drinks and everyone wins. Yeah!

Bullshit

WHAT YOU'LL NEED BESIDES BEER

....

❯ A deck of playing cards

Joining Asshole in the pantheon of "Games Named After Your Favorite Curse Words" is Bullshit. When first hearing about a game called Bullshit, many players may think it involves either (a) cow feces, or (b) unabashedly lying. Fortunately for most, this game involves the latter.

SETUP

▷ Bullshit is ideally played with at least three players.
▷ The cards are dealt out evenly among the players, facedown.
▷ All players look at their own hand but don't show it to the others.

GAME PLAY

▷ Play begins clockwise with cards being discarded facedown (which is the key) in order, starting with two and proceeding up to ace. For example, Player 1 (the first player dealt) begins by laying down a two (suit does not matter in this game). Player 2 must lay a three facedown on top of the two. Player 3 must now lay down a four, and so on up to the ace, then starting again with a two.
▷ If a player has multiples of the proper card (for example, two threes) she is allowed to lay them all down but must call out the amount she is laying down ("two threes").
▷ If a player does not have the proper card, she must "bullshit" and lay down any card(s) she wants. No "passes" are allowed.
▷ At any time a player can call "bullshit" on another player's laydown.

SCORING (DRINKING) METHOD

▷ If the player is caught bullshitting, she must pick up the entire discard pile and add it to her hand. She also takes a drink for every card she picked up.

▷ If the player was not bullshitting, the player who called her out must pick up the entire discard pile and add it to her hand. She must also take a drink for every card she picked up.

▷ A player wins by successfully discarding all of her cards.

**VARIATION:
SINNER'S BLUFF**

··············

This version adds the element of corporal punishment. If a player is caught cheating, the other players can slap her hand when retrieving their next card across the table.

COACH SAYS

In case you haven't figured it out, most of the time players are bullshitting.

Golf

WHAT YOU'LL NEED BESIDES BEER

··············

❱ A deck of playing cards

For most, going onto the golf course means spending a day wandering the green and dragging a heavy bag of clubs while sipping beer in between holes. That said, it was only a matter of time before people wised up and brought golf to the drinking table instead of bringing drinking to the golf course.

SETUP

❱ This game requires two to four players (just like in real golf, a foursome is the most fun).

❱ All players "tee off" by being dealt four cards, each placed facedown in a line.

❱ The rest of the deck is placed to the side.

❱ Players are only allowed to look at their outer two cards.

GAME PLAY

❱ Each card is given a "stroke" value as follows:
   Ace = 1 point
   Cards 2–9 = face value points
   Queen = 10 points
   King = 10 points
   Ten and jack = 0 points

❱ The goal is to make the four cards' total value be lower than the opponents' by discarding one card per turn and replacing it with a new card from the deck.

❱ Starting clockwise from the dealer, the first player takes a "swing" by drawing a card from the top of the deck. The swinger can either take a "mulligan" by replacing any of his cards with this new card or may simply discard it by placing it faceup next to the deck.

▷ In the event of a mulligan, the discarded card is placed faceup
  next to the deck.
▷ Play continues with the next player either picking up the top
  card from the discard pile or drawing a new card from the
  top of the deck.
▷ Once any player thinks he has the lowest score, that player
  knocks the table instead of drawing a card.
▷ After a knock, each player has one more turn to draw a card.
▷ When the last player is finished, everyone flips their cards
  over to reveal their scores.

SCORING (DRINKING) METHOD

▷ The player with the lowest score wins and everyone else must
  drink the difference between the winning score and his score.
  For example if the winner scores a five and you have a twelve,
  you must take seven drinks.
▷ If the player who knocked does not have the lowest score, he
  must drink double his difference.
▷ Play continues for nine or eighteen "holes," with the winner
  being the player who wins the most rounds.

Viva la fiesta! This is a very simple game of deceit to play at parties, as it requires little more than dice, a cup, and basic elementary-school math skills. Best of all, it's quick and easy to grasp, meaning a few players can orchestrate this game, play it, and still have time to celebrate Cinco de Mayo despite having no Mexican heritage!

WHAT YOU'LL NEED BESIDES BEER

••••••••••••••

> Two dice
> One red party cup (preferably the 16-ounce model)

SETUP

▷ Mexican requires at least three players, though it's also fun with more.

▷ The dice spend a lot of time in the cup, so be sure to find a cup that hasn't been used for drinking yet.

GAME PLAY

▷ The first player shakes the two dice in the cup and then turns the cup upside down on the table, keeping the dice hidden. The shaker, or "Hombre," is allowed to peek at the roll and quickly covers the dice.

▷ A roll of 2-1 is a "Mexican" and is the best roll. The next best rolls in decreasing order are as follows: 6-6, 5-5, 4-4, 3-3, 2-2, 1-1, 6-5, 6-4, 6-3, 6-2, 6-1, 5-4, 5-3, 5-2, 5-1, 4-3, 4-2, 4-1, 3-2, and 3-1 being the worst roll.

▷ After reviewing the dice, the Hombre announces her roll to everyone, keeping the dice hidden.

▷ The next player must now try to beat the Hombre's roll, or any player (even if it's not her turn) may call a "bluff."

▷ If a player calls the bluff, the Hombre must show her roll.

SCORING (DRINKING) METHOD

▷ If the Hombre was bluffing, she gets one point and must drink the total amount of the actual roll. For example, if the Hombre bluffed and said she rolled a 4-4 but actually rolled a 4-3, the hombre drinks takes seven drinks (4 plus 3 equals 7).

▷ If the Hombre was not bluffing, the accuser gets one point and must drink the total amount of the actual roll, unless the Hombre rolled a Mexican, in which case the accuser must finish her beer and is automatically eliminated from the game.

▷ If no one calls a bluff during the course of each player having a roll, the player with the best score wins the round and all the other players get one point and must drink.

▷ A player is eliminated when she gets five points. Play continues until there is only one Hombre left and this player is declared the winner. Olé!

FIFTEEN RULES OF
PROPER BEER-DRINKING ETIQUETTE

1. Always perform a toast when drinking the first beer of the day.

2. Never complain about a free beer.

3. Always have at least one six-pack in your fridge at all times.

4. Have a bottle-opening apparatus on you at all times.

5. At house parties, mark your beer so you know it's yours.

6. Never pooh-pooh another drinker's preference; everyone has their own poison.

7. At keg parties, only fill two cups at a time per person. Any more than that, get back in line.

8. If you bring beer to a party, you may drink it, but you're not allowed to take any extra home.

9. If someone buys you a beer, you must finish it.

10. If someone buys you a beer, you must buy them the next round.

11. If someone buys a round for a group, the group should toast to the buyer's health.

12. If you spill someone else's beer, you owe them a new one.

13. If someone leaves their seat to get a new beer, you must honor their claim on the space for five minutes.

14. Never bring a beer into the bathroom. It's just weird.

15. Clean up after yourself. You weren't raised in a barn. (If you were, we apologize.)

CHAPTER

7

GAMES
of
SKILL

Games of skill represent a delicious intersection of two unique forces— mind and body.

UNLIKE GAMES OF MEMORY OR STRATEGY, games of skill require an aptitude for both physical and mental challenges, demanding dexterity, focus, visual acumen, leadership, and sometimes teamwork. And since the addition of beer can dramatically impact all of the above, the appeal of these games becomes clear.

Combining beers with skills actually creates a level playing field, or in some cases, a level playing table. Players need not possess superhuman drinking ability or strength. They only need to possess a will to win, a drive to compete, and an uncanny ability to bounce something into something else.

Beer Die

Aficionados of this exhilarating game of plinks and plunks continue to debate its origins. Some camps claim it was invented in a dusty basement at the University of Colorado, while others insist it was hatched at a frat house at Colby College in Waterville, Maine. What is certain is that Beer Die is here to stay.

SETUP

▷ Beer Die requires two teams with two players per side.

▷ Both teams must sit at opposite ends of a table.

▷ One full cup of beer is placed in front of each player.

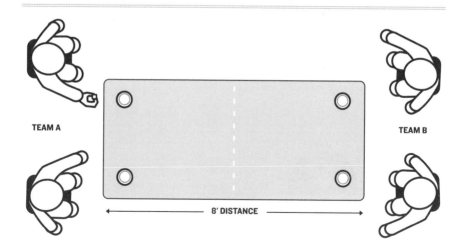

TEAM A

TEAM B

8' DISTANCE

GAME PLAY

DRINKER DICTIONARY

PDT

....

n. Short for Perfect Die Toss, this is an incredible—and incredibly difficult—shot that bounces off the back edge of the table. So instead of traveling up, it travels straight down, making it exceedingly difficult to defend.

GAME PLAY

- ▷ One player from each team rolls the die to see which team goes first. The highest roll wins.
- ▷ The first player then throws the die underhand across the table in an attempt to plunk it into one of his opponents' cups. The toss must peak at least as high as the tallest player's head to be ruled eligible.
- ▷ Beer Die is a turn-based game and each player is given a chance to throw the die, with each throw alternating between teammates and teams.

SCORING (DRINKING) METHOD

- ▷ If the thrower succeeds in getting the die into the cup, his team gets two points and the opponent who was scored upon must remove the die and chug.
- ▷ If the die hits the table, a player from the opposing team must catch the die with one hand before it hits the ground. Trapping the die against your body and catching with both hands is not permitted.
- ▷ Catching the die does not result in any points, but if the die is not caught then the throwing team gets one point and the opposing team must drink one-fifth of their beers.
- ▷ If the die bounces off the rim of a cup, the opposing team must drink half of their remaining beers.
- ▷ If the die is thrown clear off the table without bouncing, the throwing team must drink.

COACH SAYS

Think about what you say before you say it. The so-called bad numbers pop up a lot more than you might think.

- If the die lands on the table, but does not bounce off, the throwing team must drink.
- The first team to score seven points wins the game. Games must be won by two points.
- The winning team remains at the table until they lose or wet themselves.

ADDITIONAL PENALTIES

- A player must never say "seven" or "five." These are referred to as the "bad numbers." Instead, "high-bad" (seven) and "low-bad" (five) or "bizz" (five) and "buzz" (seven) are used in their place. A player caught saying either word must finish one beer every time he says a bad number.
- If a team player throws the die and it knocks one of the other team's cups over, the team that had their cup spilled must take two drinks before play can resume.
- If a player throws out of order, both players on that team must drink one-fifth of their beers.
- If a player fails to throw the die in an underhand fashion, both players on that team must drink one-fifth of their beers.
- If the die fails to travel more than one-third of the way across the table then both players on that team must drink one-fifth of their beers.

BEER DIE TIPS AND TRICKS FROM A PRO
FROM MEEKO AT BEERDIEGAME.COM

....

1. Refine your accuracy. Sinking your opponent is worth two points and can have a devastating effect on his morale.
2. Work on your catching skills. Someone who is great at catching is difficult to score against and can be just as valuable as someone who is great at throwing.
3. You can take drinks of your beer at any time during the game, and you can drink as much as you want. But you always have to drink when the rules state that you must. I try to sip a little at a time to lessen the blow if I should be sunk. Then I have less to chug.
4. Pay attention to your opponents' cups at all times. If your opponents step away from the table for whatever reason and both of their cups are still in play then you can throw at either undefended cup to try and score.
5. Shooting at the cups to try to score two points isn't always the best strategy. Sometimes it's better to go for a sure thing by shooting down the middle in between your opponents or by shooting directly at a player with subpar catching skills.

Beer Hockey

WHAT YOU'LL NEED BESIDES BEER

••••••••••••••

A true homage to Canada's national sport, this turn-based drinking game pits multiple players against one another as they attempt to score goals while simultaneously defending their crease. It's fast, fun, and unlike real hockey, it actually has a following in Nashville and Tampa Bay.

❯ One quarter or bottle cap
❯ One table
❯ One chair per player

SETUP

▷ Beer Hockey may be played with as many players as you want, although four to six is an optimal number depending upon the size of your playing surface.
▷ Players sit around a table with their beers in front of them and a quarter in the center.

GAME PLAY

▷ The player with the quarter starts the game by spinning the coin in the center of the playing surface and calling out a shooter of her choosing.

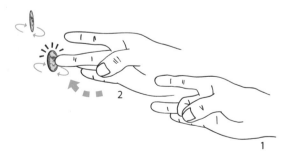

COACH SAYS

All shots must be taken by flicking the quarter. But just like in the Champagne Room, cupping and grabbing are not permitted.

- ▷ The shooter must then attempt to score a goal on her fellow players by flicking the quarter at their beers.
- ▷ The opposing players are allowed to block the front of their beers using a maximum of two fingers to cover the surface.
- ▷ If the player misses her target and the quarter is still spinning any player can shoot on any target.
- ▷ The quarter moves clockwise to the next player if a shot misses or falls off of the playing surface.

SCORING (DRINKING) METHOD

- ▷ If a player scores a goal, she must spin the quarter again and the player who allowed the goal must chug during the full duration of the spin. Other players can also try to keep the quarter in motion.
- ▷ If the player who allowed the goal finishes her beer while the quarter is still spinning she can enact "instant revenge" by slamming her empty beer on top of the quarter. She can then spin the quarter and make the player of her choosing chug her beer for the duration of the spin.
- ▷ Once the instant revenge is complete, the quarter moves clockwise to the next player and game play continues.
- ▷ If goals are scored on multiple beers in the same shot then all players who allowed goals must drink during the ensuing spin.
- ▷ Each full trip around the table counts as a single period and the player with the most goals after three periods is declared the winner.

Blowie

WHAT YOU'LL NEED BESIDES BEER

....

- A deck of playing cards
- One pint glass or plastic party cup
- An endless supply of hot air
- One table or counter

What's the best part of a birthday cake? Blowing out the candles, of course. And what's the best part of beer? Drinking it, of course. Put them together and what do you get? One of the most interesting drinking games of skill ever created, that's what.

SETUP

- ▷ Blowie is played with as many players as you want, but each player must have his own beer.
- ▷ Fill a new cup with beer and set it on a table or counter.
- ▷ Set the entire deck of cards on top of the glass.

GAME PLAY

  ▷ Players take turns blowing the cards off the deck.
  ▷ Once a player's turn is over, the next player attempts to blow.

SCORING (DRINKING) METHOD

  ▷ If one card is blown off, all the other players must take one drink from their beers.
  ▷ If more than one card is blown off, the blower must drink one gulp from his beer.
  ▷ The player who blows off the last remaining card on the glass is eliminated and must drink the glass of beer . . . plus refill it for the next round.
  ▷ If at any time the entire remaining cards are blown off, that blower is out and must drink the full glass of beer, then refill it for the next round.
  ▷ Game play restarts and continues until only one (presumably out of breath) player is left.

COACH SAYS

Tight shoulders can encase your ribs and restrict your breathing, so take a couple of deep breaths and try to loosen up prior to the game.

Caps

Anyone who carelessly tosses away her bottle caps is missing out on a chance to play one of the world's truly great drinking games. It's fun, it's easy to learn, and it's one of the few times in your life you can throw something into a stranger's drink without getting the snot beaten out of you.

WHAT YOU'LL NEED BESIDES BEER

∙∙∙∙∙∙∙∙∙∙∙∙∙∙∙

> One pint glass or plastic party cup per player
> Plenty of bottle caps
> One table
> One chair per player

SETUP

▷ Games are played with two teams of two or one.

▷ Teams sit at opposite ends of a table.

▷ One pint glass full of beer is placed in front of each player one foot from the edge of the table.

GAME PLAY

▷ Both teams take turns throwing bottle caps into their opponent's pint glass. Shots may be attempted using any method desired and can be direct or bounced. No defense is allowed in any situation.

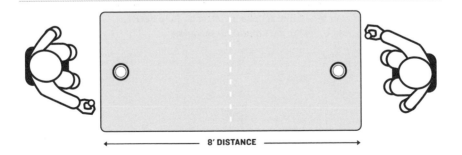

8' DISTANCE

▷ Shooters must keep their shooting elbow behind the edge of the table. It is the responsibility of the opposing team to determine if a player is shooting with her elbow over the table.

SCORING (DRINKING) METHOD

▷ Each time a shot is made, the other team gets a chance to "match" by making a shot. If no match is made, the team that made the original shot gets awarded points (see following) while the other team takes a drink.

▷ If a match is made, the team that originally made the shot tries to make a match as well. Matches can go on for as long as it takes. When a match is finally missed, that team drinks and points (see following) are awarded to the team that made the last successful shot.

▷ A direct shot can only be matched by a direct shot and a bounce can only be matched by a bounce.

▷ Games are played to eleven and must be won by two points. A 7-0 shutout is an automatic win.

▷ Points
  • Directly into the pint = 1 point
  • Bounce into the pint = 2 points

DRINKER DICTIONARY
BEER SCOOTER

....

n. The safest way of returning from a night of beer drinking. Also known as "walking" and "two feet and a heartbeat."

EXPERT CAP-TOSSING TECHNIQUES

THE DART

Hold the cap between your thumb and forefinger, keeping the knuckles pointing up and the cap lying horizontally. The power comes from a forward thrust of your elbow. Closing one eye can help you align your shot—and look like a pirate.

THE SNAP

This is the Fonzie of techniques, cool but somewhat impractical. (Wearing a leather jacket while waterskiing? Really?) To perform, place one end of the bottle cap between your thumb and middle finger, pushing down hard. Snap your fingers forcefully and the cap should shoot out . . . in some direction.

THE BREAD FOR THE DUCKS

If you play against old ladies in parks, you might be screwed because they will have this technique down. This throw is all underhand, letting the cap land as gently and softly as possible.

THE FLICK

If cool points were real and they counted in Caps, then this would be worth at least eight or nine. Balance the cap upright on your thumb with your middle and ring fingers behind it. Extend your index and pinkie to full rock-on formation. Flick the two fingers behind the cap simultaneously and launch it into victory.

Coaster Flipping

The first coasters were produced in 1880 and thirty seconds later the game of Coaster Flipping was invented. This forgotten 1950s art form is an extremely addictive game that can take over an entire bar in no time. The upside is that the bar is usually fully stocked with enough free coasters to last a lifetime. The downside is that when the stacks get too high, coasters tend to fly everywhere causing a bar fight.

WHAT YOU'LL NEED BESIDES BEER

••••••••••••••••

❱ Dozens of beer coasters
❱ Hands of a surgeon
❱ One bar counter

SETUP

▷ Games are best played with more than one person—but solo works too.
▷ Locate at least a dozen identical coasters and a bar or table with a 90-degree square edge.

GAME PLAY

▷ Place a coaster on the edge of the bar. Hang the coaster off the edge as much as possible without it falling.
▷ Hold your hand below the coaster, positioned palm down with your fingernails barely touching the bottom of the coaster.

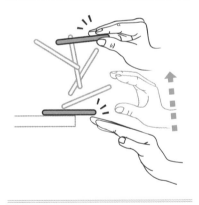

BREW FACT

A coaster was originally referred to as a "beermat" and today nearly six billion get made every year, helping protect the world's wood from the dreaded plague of beer rings.

- Bring your hand straight up quickly and push up the edge of the coaster from beneath with your fingers. The coaster will start to flip in the air.
- Catch the coaster by snatching it between your thumb and fingers, like the hand motion when doing the chicken dance.
- After each successful flip and catch, add another coaster to the stack. The challenge is to consistently flip and catch the stack in order to create the highest stack and be the winner.

SCORING (DRINKING) METHOD

THE SOPHISTICATED METHOD
- When you don't make the catch, you take a sip for every coaster you drop, with the amount resetting after every fifth coaster. For example, if you drop five coasters, you drink five sips; but if you drop six coasters, you only drink one sip.
- When you catch coasters in an increment of five, you are allowed to pass out that number of drinks to any combination of your opponents.
- For every fifteen coasters flipped, it's a social and everyone drinks.

THE SIMPLETON METHOD
- When you make a catch, you can give the number of coasters caught as drinks to any combination of opponents.
- When you miss, you need to drink as many sips as fumbled coasters.

THE HORSE METHOD
- Each player makes an attempt at flipping the coaster in increasingly difficult and dramatic moves.
- If a player cannot replicate the move, he must add one letter to the word HORSE. Once he's been forced to spell the whole word, he loses and must drink the predetermined amount.

Fire in the Hole

Drinking and cards have always gone together, but never as naturally as in Fire in the Hole. This simple but highly engrossing game challenges players to expertly toss cards into a pitcher several feet away. We like it because it involves dexterity, focus, and throwing stuff.

WHAT YOU'LL NEED BESIDES BEER

••••••••••••••

- ❱ Deck(s) of cards
- ❱ One pitcher or hat
- ❱ One table (optional)

SETUP

- ▷ Games are played with as many players as you want. The more the merrier.
- ▷ Deal the deck of cards, distributing them evenly among the players. Each player should have at least ten cards. Add additional decks as needed.
- ▷ Each player's stack is left facedown.
- ▷ Place a pitcher (or hat) in the middle of a big table or on the floor.
- ▷ Each player should stand (if using the table) or sit (if using the floor) an equal distance from the pitcher or hat.

GAME PLAY

- ▷ Players take turns drawing the top card from their stack.
- ▷ If the card is red (fire), she gets a chance to toss it into the pitcher. If the card is black, she loses her turn and the next player draws her top card.

MASTERING THE CARD TOSS

....

1. Make sure you are using newer, sturdier cards.
2. Hold the top corner of the card tightly between your index and middle fingers. The tighter you grip the card, the more control you'll have.
3. Curl your hand so the card touches the base of your wrist.
4. Keep your wrist relaxed and flick the card with a quick, fluid motion. This isn't the Hokey Pokey, so there should be little to no arm movement involved.
5. To achieve more velocity try stepping into your throw as if you were tossing a baseball.

SCORING (DRINKING) METHOD

▷ When a red card is drawn, that player must announce the value of the card. If that card is successfully thrown into the pitcher, all the other players must take a drink. If it's missed, the throwing player must take the drink.

▷ Face cards (two through nine) are worth one drink. Ten, jack, queen, and king are worth two drinks, and everyone must finish their drinks when an ace is successfully thrown.

▷ Game play continues until no cards are left.

▷ The player with the most cards in the pitcher wins.

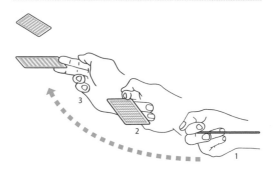

BREW FACT

The phrase "fire in the hole" can be traced back to the early twentieth century, when coal miners would shout the warning prior to igniting dynamite to loosen rock formations.

Quarters

Ask anyone to name a classic drinking game and the first one they're likely to mention is Quarters. A staple at any well-lubricated party, this lively game is believed to have originated in the United States and has since gained popularity in Canada, England, Australia, Germany, and especially South America, where it's better known as Monedita. Regardless of what you may call it, it's easy to understand why Quarters has become the go-to drinking game for revelers around the world.

WHAT YOU'LL NEED BESIDES BEER

....

- ❱ One quarter (and a few backups)
- ❱ One pitcher (amateur), or pint glass/plastic cup (pro), or shot glass (expert)

BREW FACT

The first U.S. quarter was minted in 1796 and was used in a drinking game three minutes later.

SETUP

- ▷ Games are played with as many players as you want.
- ▷ Fill the glassware with beer and set it on a table or counter.
- ▷ Make sure you have plenty of backup quarters.

GAME PLAY

- ▷ All players sit around the table and take turns trying to bounce the quarter off the table and into the glass.

PROPER SHOOTING TECHNIQUE

....

1. Choose a new quarter with no nicks or irregularities along the edges.
2. Grab the quarter between your thumb and index finger, gripping it along the edge.
3. Hold the quarter at approximately a 45-degree angle. Your hand should be no more than one foot above the playing surface for a close-range shot.
4. Bring your hand down onto the playing surface, bouncing the face or back of the quarter off the surface and into the cup or target.
5. The quarter must bounce only once, and it must go directly into the cup.
6. Don't swallow the quarter when consuming your beer unless you'd like to make change the next time you're on the can.

SCORING (DRINKING) METHOD

▷ If the quarter successfully enters the glass, the shooter commands any other player to have a drink and receives another turn.
▷ If the quarter hits the glass but does not go in, the shooter gets to reshoot.
▷ If the shooter completely misses the glass, the next player gets to shoot.
▷ If a shooter makes three quarters in a row land in the glass, he gets to make up a rule. The penalty for breaking this new rule is taking a drink.
▷ Play continues until a player has made up four rules. The fourth rule is always picking someone to drink the contents of the shooting glass.

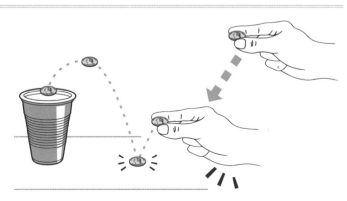

Speed Quarters

AKA NEED FOR SPEED

Want to play Quarters, but you only have three minutes before your trigonometry exam? You're in luck! You can still sneak in a quick game thanks to Speed Quarters.

**WHAT YOU'LL NEED
BESIDES BEER**

••••••••••••••

❱ Two quarters
❱ Two shot glasses
❱ One table

SETUP

▷ Games are played with as many players as you want—no less than four and preferably eight.
▷ Fill two shot glasses with beer.

GAME PLAY

▷ All players must sit or stand around a table in a circle.
▷ Play begins with two people opposite each other in the circle (or as opposite as possible). Each of the starting players gets one quarter and one shot glass set in front of them.
▷ Designate a non-shooter to yell "go!" and once yelled, the two shooters try to bounce their quarters into their glasses. Players shoot as fast as they can until their quarter makes it into the glass.

OPTIONAL QUARTER RULES

••••••••••••••

- ❭ If you point you must take a drink.
- ❭ If you swear you must take a drink.
- ❭ If you drink with your dominant hand you must take a drink.
- ❭ If you use the word "drink" you must take a drink.
- ❭ You must swap names with the player to your left. If you mix up the names or respond to your given name you must take a drink.
- ❭ You must take one gulp for each person playing the game.
- ❭ You must play the rest of the game standing on one foot.
- ❭ You must refer to yourself exclusively in the third person.
- ❭ You must take a gulp for every letter in your first name.
- ❭ You must talk like a hillbilly for the remainder of the game.

- ◷ Once a quarter gets sunk, that person passes the glass with the quarter to the person on his left.
- ◷ The person receiving the glass must remove the quarter, drink the shot, refill the glass, and immediately start shooting, attempting to sink the quarter and pass the glass as fast as possible.
- ◷ Play continues until a person gets passed both glasses—don't worry, it'll happen sooner than you think. When this occurs, that player is eliminated.
- ◷ Play continues until there is only one player remaining.

COACH SAYS

It's always a good idea to wash your quarters with dish soap and water before playing. No one knows where that 1979 quarter has been.

Distance Quarters

**AKA LONG DISTANCE,
DIALING LONG DISTANCE**

Everyone respects people who go the distance. That applies to marathon runners and mountaineers, and it will also apply to you once you master this "distant" cousin of Quarters.

WHAT YOU'LL NEED BESIDES BEER

....

- ❱ One quarter
- ❱ One pint glass or plastic party cup per player
- ❱ One table

SETUP

▷ Games are typically a one-on-one challenge between two players.

▷ One cup filled with beer is set on a table.

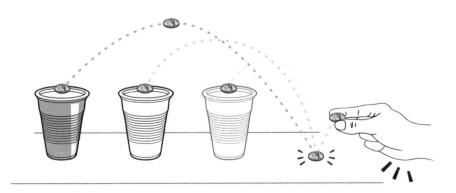

GAME PLAY

- ▷ Games are played in seven rounds.
- ▷ Each player gets two attempts to bounce the quarter on the table, trying to land it in a cup.
- ▷ If the first player misses, it's the next player's turn. If the second player sinks the quarter she wins the round.
- ▷ After each round, the glass gets pushed back six to eight inches and play continues.

SCORING (DRINKING) METHOD

- ▷ If the first player's quarter lands in the cup, the second player must also sink the quarter in the cup. If the second player misses, she loses the round and must take a drink.
- ▷ If both players sink quarters in the cup, it's considered a push and the next round begins.
- ▷ If both players miss, they both lose and must take a drink and restart the round.
- ▷ The winner starts the next round. In the event of a push, the last player in the previous round starts the next round.
- ▷ The player who wins the most rounds is the winner. In the event of a tie, a tiebreaker round is played from the farthest distance.

COACH SAYS

Striking the quarter at a greater angle—similar to skipping a rock on water—will achieve greater distance. But remember not to sacrifice accuracy for power.

Chandeliers

We generally aren't fans of spin-offs. In fact, *Joanie Loves Chachi* and *Baywatch Nights* nearly ruined the concept for us altogether until we discovered Chandeliers. This brilliant spin-off of Quarters is nearly better than the original thanks to its elegant yet rapid game play.

WHAT YOU'LL NEED BESIDES BEER

· · · · · · · · · · · · · · ·

- One quarter
- One shot glass
- One pint glass or plastic party cup per player

SETUP

- Games are played with as many players as you want. The more the merrier.
- One shot glass filled with beer is put in the center of the table.
- One cup per player is also filled with a set amount of beer (typically two to four ounces) and arranged around the shot glass in a circle, directly in front of each player.

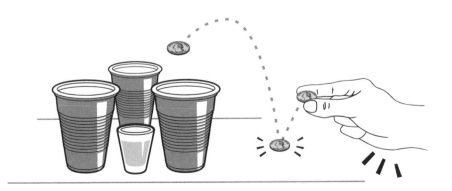

GAME PLAY

⊳ Players take turns attempting to bounce the quarter on the table, trying to land it in a player's cup or the shot glass.

SCORING (DRINKING) METHOD

⊳ If the quarter misses all the cups, it's the next player's turn.
⊳ If the quarter lands in the shooter's cup, the shooter must take a drink, and refill his cup.
⊳ If the quarter lands in another player's cup, that player must take a drink, and refill his cup.
⊳ If the quarter lands in the shot glass, each player has to drink his entire beer, and the last player to set down his empty glass must also drink the beer in the shot glass. The last player must also refill everyone's beer and is then eliminated from the game.
⊳ After each turn, the quarter is passed to the next player.
⊳ Players are eliminated when their cups get sunk three times.
⊳ Play continues until only one player remains.

COACH SAYS

You can also try playing this game with a ping-pong ball. It's a good alternative, especially if you lack the skill and finesse required to shoot with a quarter.

Baseball

What's more American than baseball? A baseball drinking game, that's what! We even posit that it's better than the actual American pastime. Not only can it be played within the comfort of your own living room rain or shine, but it also involves 50 percent less ass-patting.

WHAT YOU'LL NEED BESIDES BEER

••••••••••••••

▶ One quarter
▶ Four pint glasses or plastic party cups (regular) or four shot glasses (expert) per player
▶ One table

SETUP

▷ This game requires two teams with the same number of players, up to nine for a full lineup.
▷ Four cups are placed touching each other in a straight line. The cup line should be perpendicular to the edge of the table (leaving enough room to bounce).

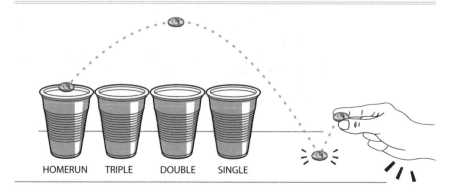

HOMERUN   TRIPLE   DOUBLE   SINGLE

GAME PLAY

▷ The game consists of nine innings in which the teams take turns "batting" in an effort to score points or "runs." A pair of turns, one at bat by each team, constitutes an inning.

▷ When batting, each team's players, in order, take turns "hitting" (bounce the quarter successfully into one of the cups). Each player gets three attempts to get a "hit" per turn.

▷ Each team gets three outs per inning.

▷ If a cup is hit or nicked but a quarter is not sunk, it is a "strike." Three strikes is one out.

▷ A quarter that is bounced and does not hit the glass or land into the cup, also called a "pop fly," is an automatic out.

SCORING (DRINKING) METHOD

▷ If a hitter strikes out or performs a pop fly, he must drink.

▷ When a player successfully makes a shot he is said to be "on base." An on-base "runner" advances to the base corresponding to the cup that was sunk. The closest cup is a single, second is a double, third is a triple, and fourth is a home run.

▷ The runner(s) also advances by the next hitter sinking a glass, which moves the on-base runner(s) the corresponding number of additional bases. For example, if the on-base runner is on first and the hitter sinks a double, the on-base runner advances to third base and the hitter advances to second.

▷ Teams are awarded one run for each on-base runner who successfully crosses home plate. For each run, the entire opposing team must take a drink.

▷ A home run is an automatic run and any on-base runners also score. In the event of a "grand slam" (a home run when the bases are loaded) the opposing team must drink their entire beers.

▷ Play continues for nine innings and the team with the most runs after nine innings is declared the winner. Unlike the shameful 2002 Major League All-Star Game, extra innings are always played in the event of a tie.

Anchorman 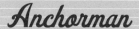 AKA LAST MAN STANDING

What does it take to be an anchorman? In the news biz, it takes graying temples, a full-bodied lip duster, and an ability to engage in senseless banter with the weather reporter. But in the world of drinking games, it takes courage, leadership, and an ability to drink twice your weight.

WHAT YOU'LL NEED BESIDES BEER

················

❭ Eight quarters
❭ One table
❭ One pitcher

SETUP

▷ Anchorman is played with two teams of four.
▷ One pitcher filled with beer is placed in the center of the table.
▷ Teams stand on opposite sides of the pitcher.
▷ Each player is given a quarter.

GAME PLAY

▷ The game begins with the first two opponents (typically the two players at the end of the table) attempting to bounce their quarters into the pitcher until a bounce successfully lands in the pitcher.
▷ Once the first quarter is successfully sunk, that team's next player gets to shoot. This process continues sequentially until all team members have successfully sunk their quarters.
▷ In the event that the last two opponents' quarters were sunk at the exact same time, the game is decided with a rematch.

SCORING (DRINKING) METHOD

▷ The first team to get all four quarters into the pitcher wins.
▷ The losing team must chug the pitcher in the same order in which they shot, with the last person being the "Anchorman."
▷ The Anchorman must finish whatever is left in the pitcher.

Moose

**AKA MOOSE CUP, BEERWINKLE,
ICE ICE BABY**

WHAT YOU'LL NEED BESIDES BEER

••••••••••••••

❱ One plastic ice cube tray
❱ One quarter
❱ One table
❱ One pint glass or plastic party cup

Think ice cube trays are just for making ice? Think again. All it takes is a playful spirit and a whole lot of alcohol to transform those little chunks of molded plastic into the centerpiece of a truly entertaining drinking game for generations of college kids.

SETUP

🜂 Games are played with as many players as you want, but no less than three.

🜂 One standard ice cube tray is placed on a table perpendicular to the end of the table (facing away from the players) and about two feet in from the end of the table (leaving enough room to bounce).

🜂 The far side of the tray is designated the "give" side and the near side is designated the "take" side.

🜂 One cup full of beer, called the "moose cup," is placed at the far end of the tray.

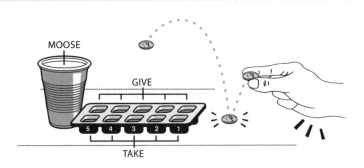

GAME PLAY

▷ Players take turns trying to bounce the quarter into the ice cube tray.

▷ Each cube has a value, the closest being one, the next being two, and so on. Typically there are eight to ten cubes in a tray.

SCORING (DRINKING) METHOD

▷ When the quarter lands in a cube on the "give" side, the shooter earns points based on the cube's value and also distributes that many sips to any combination of players. For example, if the quarter lands in the third cube, three points are awarded and three drinks are given out to players in any amount—two to Player 1 and one to Player 2, or two to Player 2 and one to Player 1, or three to Player 1, or . . . you get it.

▷ When the quarter lands in the ice cube tray on the "take" side, the shooter has to drink according to the cube's value it landed into, and those points are deducted. For example, if the quarter lands in the fourth cube, four points are deducted and four drinks must be taken.

▷ If the quarter lands on the ice cube tray but doesn't fall into a cube, it's a social and everyone drinks.

▷ If the quarter lands in the "moose cup," every player has to put their hands to their heads, mimicking antlers, and yell "moose!" The last person to yell "moose!" has to drink the moose cup. The moose cup gets refilled and replaced after each "moose!"

▷ Play continues until someone scores eleven points.

BREW FACT

Moose with antlers tend to have more sensitive hearing than moose that don't, so watch what you say if one is in the next room.

CHAPTER

8

GAMES
— of —
NO SKILL
AND NO
STRATEGY

(BUT THAT ARE STILL
REALLY FUN
— *and* —
YOU SHOULD TRY
TO PLAY THEM ANYWAY)

Oftentimes, the modern world can get too complicated.

THAT'S WHY PEOPLE STILL go camping—because they want to reestablish one of the most important connections of all: the connection between man and nature. In that regard, drinking games of absolutely no skill or strategy are much like the drinking man's version of getting back to nature.

There's a beauty and simplicity that comes from removing all the convolution and challenges that may come from a complicated drinking game and getting back to the basics: you and your beer. It's this Zen-like awareness of one's connection to the present, the universe, and the delicious bubbly liquid that make these games so enticing.

What follows is a survey of some simple but fun games that require nothing more than some beer, some drinking buddies, and some luck.

Acey Deucey

WHAT YOU'LL NEED BESIDES BEER

....

> A deck of playing cards

Unlike a lot of other card games out there, Acey Deucey is a game that can potentially screw over the dealer just as easily as it can the player, making it a deceptively fun way to force people to drink.

SETUP

- This is a two-player, head-to-head challenge played in a best-of-seven series
- Both players are dealt two cards faceup and one card facedown. All cards are ranked by their face value except for aces. Two is the lowest and king is the highest.

GAME PLAY

- If an ace is dealt for the first faceup card, it's considered the "lowest" card. If an ace is dealt for the second faceup card, it's considered the "highest" card.
- The object is now to guess whether the facedown card will fall "inside" or "outside" the two cards. For example, if the player is dealt a two and a four, only a three is considered inside and everything else is outside.
- After both sets are dealt, both players shout their guesses and flip their cards simultaneously.

?

SCORING (DRINKING) METHOD

▷ If both players are correct, it's a tie and no one drinks.
▷ If both players are incorrect, it's a tie and both players drink.
▷ If one player is correct, the opponent must drink and he loses the round.
▷ If a player's faceup cards are of equal value, it's an automatic win and the opposing player drinks.
▷ If both players' faceup cards are of equal value, it's a tie, both players drink, and the deck must get reshuffled.
▷ Play continues until someone wins four rounds.

Beer Roulette

WHAT YOU'LL NEED BESIDES BEER

....

❱ An empty cooler

Beer Roulette throws caution to the wind and leaves the dryness of a player's clothes in the hands of luck alone. Borrowing from the infamous Russian roulette, this game teaches players about the importance of decisions—and of bringing a change of clothes.

SETUP

▷ This game works best with six players and a six-pack of cans (no bottles).

▷ You need one beer for each player.

GAME PLAY

▷ Shake one can vigorously, then put it back with the others so no one knows which one is shaken. If there are more than six people playing, shake two cans. Add an extra shaken can to the mix for every six players. Once the cans are shaken, throw all of the cans (shaken and unshaken) into a cooler.

▷ Each player picks a can and holds it up to the side of her head with the mouth of the can facing her head.

▷ At once, everyone opens their cans.

SCORING (DRINKING) METHOD

▷ The players who weren't sprayed win and celebrate by drinking their beers and laughing at the loser.

Boat Race

AKA BEERELAY, TEAM CHUG, CANOE

This is a team-based event once reserved for Ivy League crew teams but now everyone from the GED graduate to the PhD candidate can play.

SETUP

- Two teams of equal numbers line up across from each other, standing at a table or sitting on the floor. Traditional matchups are five vs. five, seven vs. seven, or nine vs. nine.
- Each player must place a drinking vessel (cup, glass, mug, etc.) full of beer in front of them. Whichever vessel is used, it must be the same for all players.

GAME PLAY

- The game begins with the first two opponents at the end of the table partaking in a toast, which consists of tapping their cups, lowering them down to hit the table, then back up to drink.
- Once the beer is consumed, the player must invert the empty vessel over his or her head.
- After the cup is proven to be empty, the next player grabs his cup and consumes the beer as quickly as possible and then inverts it over his head.
- This continues down the line.

SCORING (DRINKING) METHOD

- Simply put: the team that finishes first wins.
- Empty vessels must remain held over each competitor's head until the race is over. If any beer spills, that player is considered "overboard" and their team is automatically disqualified.

WHAT YOU'LL NEED BESIDES BEER

....

- A drinking vessel for each player
- A table (optional)

ULTIMATE BOAT RACE

....

Nonconformists will agree that drinking out of a cup can be boring. If you want to add a challenge to this game, have all the players drink out of Frisbees to test the limits of their drinking ability.

Case Race

Possibly one of the biggest, most impressive feats of fortitude is the Case Race. Its pure competitiveness is matched only by its gluttony.

WHAT YOU'LL NEED BESIDES BEER

> Intestinal fortitude

SETUP

▷ This is best played by at least two teams of three players each. More is allowed, as long as both teams have the same number.

DRINKER DICTIONARY
BREAKING THE SEAL

v. The first urination of the night. Can lead to in-game distractions if not properly managed.

GAME PLAY

▷ Each team must work together to finish their case of beer.

SCORING (DRINKING) METHOD

▷ The first team to finish wins.
▷ Nothing more to it.

HOW TO HOLD IT

During intense drinking games, neither failure nor urination is an option. Here are four tips to stave off number one.

I. CROSS YOUR LEGS ONLY IF STANDING. This can help close off the urethra and limit movements that might, um, shake things out. But do not cross if you are seated. This puts extra pressure on your bladder.

2. SIT UP, BUT CHILL OUT. The key is to relieve tension before you accidentally, um, relieve yourself. So sit upright but let your lower abdomen tilt forward slightly, again taking pressure off your bladder.

3. FOCUS AND FIDGET. Subtle, unjarring leg and arm movements are a way to help distract you from the situation down there.

4. NOT SO FAST. Some recent research shows that people needing to go made better strategic, long-term decisions compared to their recently peed peers.

High Low

Easily one of the most basic games out there, High Low is easy to learn, nearly impossible to argue over, and provides a stage for ample beer consumption. A mastery of this game is essential as there will always be some point in the night when a game that involves thought, strategy, or skill is just too much to muster.

SETUP

◗ This game requires at least two players, but it doesn't prove entertaining for groups bigger than six.
◗ Players sit around a yet-to-be dealt deck of cards with a full beer in front of them.

GAME PLAY

◗ One player is dealt a card. The object is to guess whether the next card in the deck will be higher or lower than the dealt card.
◗ After three or more successful guesses, the player may pass to the next player.
◗ Once the player passes, the next player starts with the last card the previous player left behind.

COACH SAYS

The strategy is to build up a lot of cards and then pass to the next player, making it harder for them and causing them to potentially take more drinks.

Instead of High Low, you can make things quicker and easier by just playing Red Black. The rules are the same but instead of guessing if the next card will be higher or lower, you just guess if the next card will be red or black. This quicker version is perfect for those frequent bathroom break intermissions.

SCORING (DRINKING) METHOD

▷ If a player guesses wrong, she drinks for every card that is turned over. For example if there are two cards showing and she guesses wrong on the next turn, she must take two sips.

▷ After each wrong guess, play is reset and starts from the last card turned.

▷ If a card of equal value is turned, it's a social and everyone drinks. An equal card is considered a do-over for the guessing player.

▷ Play continues until no one wants to play anymore. Everyone wins!

COACH SAYS

Wesley Snipes said you should always bet on black. He's right, if by "always" he means "half the time" and by "bet" he means "pay your taxes."

···· ➡ **LOW**   ···· ➡ **HIGH**   ···· ➡ **LOW**   ···· ➡ **PASS**

Horse Race

Horse Race is a game that just naturally generates excitement, thanks to the bets and the stakes behind those bets. Let your inner bookie out.

WHAT YOU'LL NEED BESIDES BEER

....

▶ A deck of playing cards

SETUP

▷ This game requires at least four players, but the more the merrier.

▷ Pull out the four aces from the deck. These are the "horses."

▷ Lay out the "track" starting with the "gate" by laying the four aces faceup and side by side at one end of the table. Next, set up the "lanes" by laying six random cards facedown in a straight line perpendicular to the aces.

GAME PLAY

▷ Before the race begins, each player chooses his horse by its suit. When more than four players are playing, players may have the same suit but only after all four suits have already been picked once.

▷ Each player makes a "bet" on his horse. A bet is a set amount of drinks, typically between one and five but you can go as high as a full beer.

▷ Once all the bets are in, the announcer flips over the remaining cards in the deck one at a time. The suit of the card flipped corresponds to the aces in the game.

▷ Whatever suit is pulled, the corresponding ace is advanced by one card on the track.

▷ Continue flipping cards until one of the horses goes past the final card in the lane to win.

SCORING (DRINKING) METHOD

▷ If a player picks a winning horse, he gets to distribute his bet (drinks).

▷ Losing players must drink their own bets, plus whatever else a winning player might hand out to them.

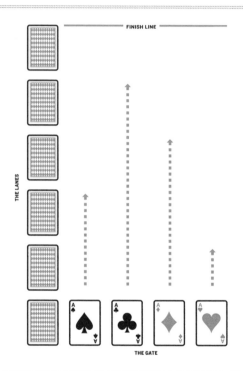

COACH SAYS

If you love to bet and love to drink, then add some more excitement to this game by side betting exactas, quinellas, trifectas, and super-fectas. If you know what those bets are then you should try it. If you don't, then stick to the basic straight bet—it's still fun.

Kings

They say that chess is the game of kings. We say that Kings is the game of kings. Versatile enough to be played by anyone from a prince to a pauper, it's a royal good time. We've run out of mildly amusing puns about kings, so you'll need to trust us that this classic has been passed down for many generations for a reason.

WHAT YOU'LL NEED BESIDES BEER

....

> A deck of playing cards
> A big empty cup

SETUP

> Kings is best played with three to eight individuals.
> Spread an entire deck of playing cards face-down around the empty cup.

GAME PLAY

> Taking turns and rotating clockwise, players draw a card and follow the rule for each card (explained in the Scoring section).
> For each king drawn, that player must also fill one-third of the center cup with her beer.
> Once the fourth king is drawn, the game is over and the player to draw the fourth king loses and must drink the now-full center cup.

SCORING (DRINKING) METHOD

For each card picked a rule must be followed:
> Ace = waterfall. The player who drew the card starts drinking, so then does everyone. When the person who drew the card stops drinking, the person to their right stops. This continues around the whole table.

MAKE A RULE CHEAT SHEET

....

Here are some "Make a Rule" suggestions for your game.

TIME-OUT: If you say another person's name, you must put your head on the table, in "time-out," until someone else breaks the rule.

POTTY MOUTH: If you swear, you drink.

ACCENT TIME: You must use the accent assigned to you. Break character, you drink.

IN MY PANTS: You must complete every sentence with said phrase, and if you don't, you drink—in my pants.

POINTLESS: Anyone who points, you guessed it, must drink.

BOX HEAD: Fashion a hat out of an empty case of beer. You must wear it until a jack is drawn.

DRINK DRANK DRUNK: None of those words can be uttered. If one is, you must ~~drink~~ imbibe.

▷ Five = guys. All male players must drink. (If playing with all females you can play "Give Five" and distribute five drinks in any combination. You must also call a male and ask him and his friends to come over.)

▷ Six = chicks. All female players must drink. (If playing with all males you can play "Give Six" and distribute six drinks in any combination. You must also call a female and ask her and her friends to come over.)

▷ Seven = heaven. All players must point up. The last player to point must drink.

▷ Eight = mate. Pick another player to be your "drinking mate." Anytime either player has to drink, her mate must drink too.

▷ Nine = bust a rhyme. Say a phrase, then all the other players in turn must say a phrase that rhymes with the original. The first player who can't come up with a phrase, says a phrase that doesn't rhyme, or repeats a phrase, must drink.

▷ Ten = category. Pick a category and the other players must say items from that category. The first player who can't think of an item, says something not in the category, or repeats an item, must drink.

▷ Jack = make a rule. Create a rule that all the players must obey until the end of the game.

▷ Queen = question. Ask any player a question. That player must answer the question then turn to someone else and ask a different question and so on. If a player does not ask a question, cannot think of a question quickly, or repeats a question, she must drink.

▷ King = thumbs. At any time during the game, you can place your thumb on the table. The last person to put her thumb on the table must drink.

Three Man

It's generally a good idea to avoid doing arithmetic when drinking, unless of course you're playing Three Man. This game combines the thrill of boozing with the challenge of simple addition to create a game that anyone with a liver and a first-grade education can enjoy. Take a look at the rules and we're sure you'll agree it all adds up to a ton of fun.

WHAT YOU'LL NEED BESIDES BEER

- Two dice
- One table
- One chair per player

SETUP

- Three Man is played with as many players as you want. The more the merrier.
- Players sit around a table with their drinks in front of them and a pair of dice in the center.

GAME PLAY

- Everyone takes turns rolling a single die until someone rolls a three. This person becomes the Three Man.
- The game then proceeds around the circle in a clockwise direction with players rolling two dice at a time.
- The dice are only passed from one person to the next when a player rolls a number combination that does not require drinking.

SCORING (DRINKING) METHOD

In Three Man, there is no simple roll of the dice. The following is a list of dice scores and their corresponding actions.

▷ Three: Whenever the numbers on the dice add up to three, the Three Man must drink. He may then pass his title onto the player of his choosing.

▷ Seven: Whenever the numbers on the dice add up to seven, the person to the right of the roller must have a drink.

▷ Nine: Whenever the numbers on the dice add up to nine, the person across from the roller must have a drink.

▷ Ten: Whenever the numbers on the dice add up to ten, everyone must have a drink.

▷ Eleven: Whenever the numbers on the dice add up to eleven, the person to the left of the roller must have a drink.

▷ Four and one: Whenever a player rolls a four and a one, he becomes the Thumb Master. The Thumb Master can place his thumb on the table at any time during the game and everyone else must do the same. The last person to put his thumb on the table must have a drink. The Thumb Master retains the title until another player rolls a four and a one.

▷ Doubles: Whenever a player rolls doubles he gives the dice to another player of his choosing. If that player rolls doubles, he gives the dice to another player of his choosing. If not, he must take a drink.

Up the River, Down the River

AKA HELL YEAH!, STINKY FINGERS, GET FRED

Remember that song "Proud Mary"? The one Tina Turner sang about "Rollin', rollin', rollin' down the river"? That song was written about Up the River, Down the River. Okay, maybe it wasn't, but it should have been. Easily one of the most nautically themed drinking games out there, it builds on those matching skills you honed during many a childhood game of "Memory."

WHAT YOU'LL NEED BESIDES BEER

••••••••••••••

> One deck of playing cards (maybe two)

COACH SAYS

If you're playing with six or more players, you're gonna need two decks of cards.

SETUP

- ▷ You will need at least three players to join you on this expedition.
- ▷ Each player (including the dealer) is dealt four cards faceup arranged in a straight horizontal line in front of them.
- ▷ The remaining deck is placed in a pile in front of the dealer.

GAME PLAY

- ▷ There are four "up the river" (take a drink) rounds and four "down the river" (give a drink) rounds.
- ▷ The game begins "up the river" when the dealer flips over the first card off the top of the remaining deck.

SCORING (DRINKING) METHOD

▷ Any player with the same card value that was flipped (suit doesn't matter) must take one drink.

▷ If a player has more than one card that matches the flipped card, she must take a drink for each match she has.

▷ After each "up the river" turn, the dealer then flips over the next card from the deck and the same rules apply. For each turn, however, the amount of drinks increases by one. Turn 1 = take one drink per match, turn 2 = two drinks, turn 3 = three drinks, turn 4 = four drinks.

▷ After the four "up the river" turns, the game reverses to "down the river."

▷ The dealer flips over the next card in the deck and any player who has a match can now give out four drinks in any combination. If a player has more than one match, she gives out four drinks for each match she has.

▷ After each "down the river" turn, the dealer continues to turn over the next card from the deck and the same rules apply. However, after each round, the amount of drinks given decreases by one. Turn 1 = give four drinks per match, turn 2 = three drinks, turn 3 = two drinks, turn 4 = one drink.

▷ Play starts over and continues until everyone quits.

Wizard's Staff

When the Dungeons & Dragons generation came of age, it was only inevitable that they would develop their own homegrown drinking game. And while playing Wizard's Staff is benign fun, it could lead participants down a slippery slope to LARP and even Comic-Con. So please play Wizard's Staff responsibly.

WHAT YOU'LL NEED BESIDES BEER

....

❭ A roll of duct tape

SETUP

▷ This can be played by two to two hundred people at once. (If you do play with two hundred people, please invite us at www.TheBookofBeerAwesomeness.com.)

GAME PLAY

▷ Players start by drinking a can of beer. Once finished, tape the empty can under a new full can of beer.

▷ Drink the new can of beer. Once that one is empty, tape a third new, full can to the top of the stack and so on.

SCORING (DRINKING) METHODS

▷ The goal of the Wizard's Staff is to see how many cans can be stacked and taped. As the cans add up, it gets more difficult—especially for shorter drinkers. The longest staff, obviously, wins.

VARIATION

▷ Another variation has players compete to create a ten-can staff and become a "white wizard." Each white wizard does actual battle with the other wizards, trying to break his opponent's staff to become champion.

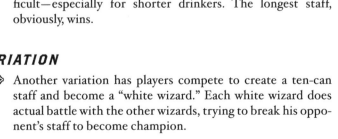

CHAPTER

9

BEER
DRINKING
SPORTS

The difference between a game and sport is abundantly clear.

BUT IF WE NEED TO EXPLAIN IT, you've obviously never experienced the adrenaline coursing through your veins as your ball hurdles through the night air. Or as your cup teeters on the edge of the table.

These are not drinking games. Sure, they involve drinking and they are played in a game-like fashion. But rest assured these are beer *sports* through and through.

Beer sports are best experienced firsthand. Only then can you know the thrill of victory and the agony of drinking in defeat. In the meantime, here is an overview of all the best of beer sports in handy book form.

DRINKING GAMES VS. BEER SPORTS

Here we break down details of what makes a beer sport different . . . and badass.

DRINKING GAMES	DRINKING SPORTS
Losing is a bummer	Losing is not an option
Minimal physical activity	Pitting is guaranteed
Brings friends together	Alienates friends forever
Someone may get embarrassed	Someone may pull a hammy
Competitors hold beer	Competitors hold grudges
Anyone can win	Only the strong can survive
Results will be forgotten in moments	Results will be discussed for years to come
At least one person will be shirtless	At least one person will be wearing a uniform
It's better to be lucky than good	It's better to be good than lucky
Results in empties	Results in trophies

Beer Pong AKA PONG, BEIRUT

Cue the music (think "Also Sprach Zarathustra" by Richard Strauss, better known as Ric Flair's theme song) and fireworks because the king has entered the arena. Welcome to the alpha beer sport. Imagine the head-to-head intensity of a prizefight, the strategy of a chess match, and the shameless self-congratulation of an NFL touchdown dance. Now mix in the pressure of a game-winning free throw and the alcohol tolerance of a Russian parliamentary meeting. That's Beer Pong.

WHAT YOU'LL NEED BESIDES BEER

> 20 plastic party cups for beer
> 2 beer pong balls (aka table tennis balls)
> 2 cups filled with water
> 1 table

SETUP

▷ Beer Pong is a team sport of skill. There are two two-player teams, a table, and ten cups set up on each end of the table.

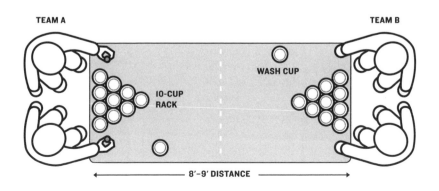

TEAM A

TEAM B

WASH CUP

IO-CUP RACK

8'–9' DISTANCE

▷ Ten plastic cups are arranged in a pyramid at each end of the table. These cups are filled with a mutually agreed-upon volume of a mutually agreed-upon beverage. Two additional cups of water are furnished for cleaning purposes.

GAME PLAY

▷ The two teams stand on opposing sides of the table and attempt to throw, bounce, or otherwise propel a regulation table tennis ball into their opponents' cups on the opposite side of the table.

▷ The two teams alternate turns, with each member of the team throwing a single ball on each turn. If both players successfully "sink" their balls in a single turn, they get their balls back and get to shoot again—this is called a "brinkback." If only one or no balls are sunk, the turn is over, and the other team throws their two balls.

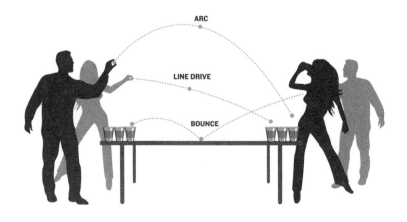

SCORING (DRINKING) METHOD

> ▷ When a player successfully throws a ball into the opponent's cup, the opponent must remove the ball and drink the cup's contents. Empty cups are removed from play. The contest is over when one of the teams no longer has any cups in front of them.

> ▷ Unlike in real life, there is always an opportunity for a second chance in Beer Pong, and it's called rebuttals. Once the final cup has been sunk, the losing team is allowed one additional turn to attempt to remove all their remaining cups. The losing team's last cup is not removed until rebuttals have failed.

> ▷ If more than one cup remains on one side when the final cup has been sunk, the Gentleman's Rule goes into effect: each player gets to shoot until she misses. This means a single player can sink all the remaining cups so long as she doesn't miss. Once she misses, her partner gets the same opportunity. Once her partner misses, the game is ruled over.

> ▷ If only one cup remains when the final cup has been sunk and the opponents sink their last cup in one turn, the rebutting team only gets one shot. If the opponents sink their last cup on their second turn, the rebutting team gets two shots.

> ▷ If, at the end of the rebuttal, the rebutting team does not make *all* the remaining cups, they lose and the game is over.

> ▷ The losing team must consume its remaining cups as well as its opponents' remaining cups. It is up to the losing team to determine the distribution of beverages among the players.

> ▷ If the rebutting team sinks all their remaining cups, then the game goes into overtime. New racks with three cups per side are set up, and the team that sunk the last cup starts first with the balls. Original rules apply. The number of overtimes is unlimited.

DRINKER DICTIONARY

BEERACLE

. . . .

n. A miracle that is caused by almighty beer, e.g., making ten straight cups in a game of Beer Pong.

MASTERING THE SPORT

The following section will help you go from a "chucker" (a no-game-having-newbie) to a "ringer."

THE GRIP

The ball grip is one of the game's most critical elements. It's what controls accuracy, speed, and ball spin. When analyzing form, this is where the rubber meets the road—or more accurately, where the fingertips meet the plastic.

THE TRADITIONAL GRIP AKA DA GRIP, THE BASIC OVERHAND, BOB

The ball is held between the thumb and forefinger, resting on the middle finger for stability. The release comes with a quick snap of the wrist to produce slight backspin. It works with all stances and shooting styles. Popular, universal, effective. This grip is a must for anyone trying to play the game. In short, this is the missionary position of ball grips.

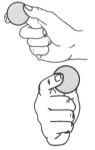

THE TRIGGER GRIP AKA THE OVERHAND HOOK, THE BUSTA KAPPA KAPPA

A variation on the Traditional. The ball is held between the tip of the thumb and the entire index finger. The middle finger remains down, resting for future post-game use. Since it does not generate much spin, this grip can cause shots to run wild—especially during outdoor play.

THE GRANNY GRIP AKA THE LOB, THE SEMI-PRO

The ball is gently cradled in your hand like a delicate flower. It is then tossed in a smooth underhanded swing. When mastered, the toss will create no ball spin whatsoever, which makes this a good opening shot for a full rack. Fortunately for this grip, style points are not factored in the game.

THE SHOT

The Beer Pong shot is much more than the mere sum of its parts. It's a graceful orchestration of muscles, joints, and cartilage working together under the watchful conductor of your brain. To help you execute this Byzantine process more smoothly, we've created a simple acronym to encapsulate the totality of this world-class technique. We call it our BEEER method.

 B = Balance: Make sure you are balanced before you attempt a shot.

 E = Eyes: Direct your eyes to a specific cup while you shoot.

 E = Elbow: Keep your elbow in toward your body when shooting.

 E = Extend: Extend your arm as you release and follow through.

 R = Remember: The first four points are, like, kinda worth remembering.

YOUR JOURNEY TO BEER PONG MASTERY HAS JUST BEGUN

Let's face it—we could probably write an entire book on just Beer Pong alone. Wait a minute, we actually did! It's *The Book of Beer Pong—The Official Guide to the Sport of Champions*. Check out TheBookofBeerPong.com to learn more.

COACH SAYS

Throw the ball with a smooth, fluid motion. Don't flick or jerk it like a madman. You don't need to hurl the ball with great force to sink a cup.

Beer Darts

Darts and beer have a long storied history—rich with erudite conversation in British pubs. But when hardened Midwesterners and Canadians took it over, it transformed into the ultimate New World drinking sport: beer in cans, asses in seats, and projectiles in human flesh (possibly).

WHAT YOU'LL NEED BESIDES BEER

••••••••••••••

❱ 2 seats (lawn chair, cooler, tree stump, etc.)
❱ A few standard lightweight metal darts
❱ 2 pieces of cardboard for backstop (optional)

WARNING:
PLAY BEER DARTS AT YOUR OWN RISK

••••••••••••••••

This is not some ironic reverse psychology that is really secretly tempting you to participate in this possibly puncture-inducing pastime. And that alliteration in the previous sentence was not an attempt to make it sound cool, either. This game can be dangerous. Don't say we didn't warn you.

SETUP

▷ Beer Darts is best played between two people.
▷ Place seats twenty feet apart (ten feet apart if playing at night when vision is limited).
▷ The players grab seats, facing each other.
▷ An unopened can of beer is placed at each player's feet.
▷ If playing in teams, add more chairs and more beers.
▷ All players must be seated or in a squatting stance with at least one can of unopened beer directly in front of them.

GAME PLAY

▷ The player with the dart propels it toward his opponent's can—and hopefully not his opponent's shin.

▷ After the throw, the drinking mandate is decided, as specified in the following section, and the receiving player becomes the thrower.

▷ Play continues indefinitely or until someone taps out.

SCORING (DRINKING) METHOD

▷ There are no points, only drinking mandates, which are "awarded" to the receiver as follows:

▷ If the dart touches the can but does not puncture it (a "tick"), the player takes one sip of beer.

▷ If the dart punctures the can, the player must drink to the level of the hole.

▷ If the can is punctured three times, the beer must be fully consumed and the game is over.

▷ If the dart enters the mouth of the can and its shaft drops down, the beer must be fully consumed and the game is over.

▷ If the dart enters the body of the opponent, the thrower must fully consume his beer.

Beer Run

Running and beer have been closely linked throughout history. There is running out to get beer, running after people who took your beer, and of course, the runs from drinking beer. But the purest form is the classic Beer Run drinking sport.

GAME PLAY VARIATIONS

....

VARIATION #1: BEER MILE
This relay version involves four-player teams and a standard quarter-mile track. The race starts with the first competitor on each team pounding a cold one, running one lap around the track, and then cleanly handing off the empty can to the next teammate. This drink, run, and pass is then repeated three more times.

VARIATION #2: BIERKASTENLAUF
It means "beer crate–running" and that's, well, exactly what it is. Popular in German-speaking and German-drinking countries, it is a race among teams of two people carrying a crate of beer. Twenty bottles and ten kilometers. You do the math.

VARIATION #3: HASH RUN
In 1938, a group of British servicemen in Malaysia created a running and drinking club. Today, close to two thousand chapters worldwide continue the tradition. One runner (the hare) sets out, leaving a Byzantine running path with flour or chalk marks. The pack (the hashers) must follow the twists, turns, and dead ends to reach the goal: a bar or drinking area.

SETUP

▷ Like any race, Beer Run is best with more than one person.
▷ Starting and finish lines must all be predetermined.

GAME PLAY

▷ Drink a beer.
▷ Run.
▷ For more details, see the game play variations on the left.

SCORING (DRINKING) METHOD

▷ The first person to cross the finish line with the contents of their stomach intact wins.

Cornhole

If you've ever been to a tailgate, a backyard barbecue, or college, then you've witnessed the awesomeness known as Cornhole. Cornhole is more than just tossing a bag into a hole. Cornhole has transcended the label of "lawn game" to become an important social bridge. The game gathers the rich and the poor to a common cause. Neighbors get to know neighbors, unknowns become knowns. God bless America and her beautiful Cornhole.

WHAT YOU'LL NEED BESIDES BEER

••••••••••••••

- ❯ 2 Cornhole boards
- ❯ 4 to 8 Cornhole bags (two different colors), see Brew Fact on page 192

SETUP

- ▷ Traditionally played with two teams with two players per team but the game can also be played as singles or multiplayer teams.
- ▷ Position the Cornhole boards at the appropriate distance apart: 27 feet front edge to front edge of the board for official competitive regulation; 24 feet for casual or novice players; or any distance you want for the fun of it (see illustration on page 188).

THE CORNHOLE BOARD

You can make one (expert), or just buy one (easy).

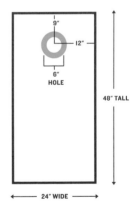

TOP VIEW

9"

12"

6"
HOLE

48" TALL

24" WIDE

12" TALL

3" THICK

SIDE VIEW

GAME PLAY

▷ Players on the same team stand directly across from one another and stay in this position for the entire match. Partners do not stand on the same side or diagonally across from each other (see illustration below). If playing singles, both players toss or pitch from the same side and switch sides after each turn.

▷ Each team gets their own colored bags. Players pitch the bags at the Cornhole board located across from them.

▷ Two opponents from the same side take turns pitching, four bags each per round. After each round, play switches to the opposite side. Play begins with the player of the team that scored the previous round.

▷ Players must throw from behind the front edge of the board to avoid a foot fault. A foot fault results in the bag being removed from the board (if applicable). The same rule applies if a player throws out of turn.

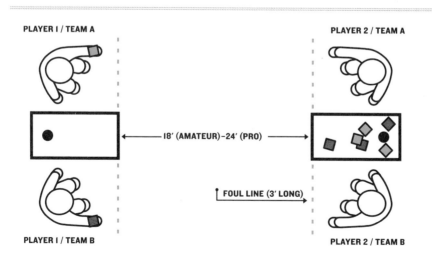

PLAYER 1 / TEAM A   PLAYER 2 / TEAM A

◀── 18' (AMATEUR)–24' (PRO) ──▶

↑ FOUL LINE (3' LONG)

PLAYER 1 / TEAM B   PLAYER 2 / TEAM B

◊ Bags must land and stay on the board (without touching the ground) or go completely through the hole to score. Knocking an opponent's bag off the board is always legal.

◊ To determine who starts the match, one player from each team throws a single bag shoot-out, the bag closest to the hole wins. Repeat in the event of a tie.

SCORING (DRINKING) METHOD

◊ A bag in the hole is called a "cornhole" and earns three points.

◊ A bag on the board is called a "woody" and earns one point.

◊ A bag that completely misses the board and/or touches the ground results in zero points and the shooter must drink. A foot fault also results in zero points and the shooter must drink.

◊ At the end of each round, the losing side must drink the amount of points they lost the round by. For example, losing by three points means each losing player must take three drinks.

◊ Points cancel each other out.
  • For example: The red team (red bags) has three bags on the board (three points) and one bag in the hole (three points) totaling six points.
  • The blue team (blue bags) has three bags on the board (three points) and one bag off the board (zero points).
  • The red team wins the round scoring three points (six points for the red team minus three points for the blue team equals three points net for the red team) and the blue team must take three drinks.

◊ The first team to get to twenty-one points wins the game. Getting 13-0 is considered an automatic win or "shucking," and the losing team must finish their beers.

Cornhole Drinker Dictionary

As you can see, Cornhole is a very distinct sport, and like all things distinct, a specific vocabulary is inevitable.

AIRMAIL: A cornhole—nothing but hole.

BLOCKIN': A player blocking the hole by the position of one of his bags.

CANDY CORN: A short shot—this one didn't make it to the board.

DIRTY: When a bag hits the ground before reaching the board.

FAULTIN': A foot fault; stepping past the front of the board.

CORNHOLE: A three-point shot, one that ends up in the hole on its own or with help, they all count.

CORNZIZZLE: When a player makes four cornholes in one round.

SHUCKED: A team or player who is beaten 13–0 as in "You've been shucked—now drink up, son!"

LIPPER: A woody hanging on the lip of the hole and is ready to drop in.

SLICK WOODY: Cornhole, this one slides into the hole.

STANKER: Any foul bag such as a "dirty," "faultin," or "candy corn"—zero point value.

WOODY: A one-point shot landing and staying on the board surface.

MASTERING THE GAME

Perfecting a proper pitching technique is the only way to accurately and consistently get in the hole (that's what she said). Here is a rundown of the most popular grips and stances.

PITCHING GRIPS

WAD AKA NEWBIE, FOLD

Most commonly used by beginners. Player grabs bag as if it is a ball and tries pitching it. This is an inconsistent grip often resulting in inaccurate pitches.

PINCHY AKA SLING, FLING

Player pinches the corner or side of the bag and flips it. Fairly safe shot for having your bag land on the board resulting in a woody.

CLASSIC AKA PANCAKE, FRISBEE

This grip is used by most professionals, with the thumb on top of bag and four fingers underneath. Player is attempting to get bag to fly flat with a little spin. Gives players the most options for bag performance, by helping to slide to the hole more accurately.

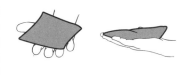

HOW TO IMPROVE YOUR CORNHOLING
BY FRANK GEERS, FOUNDER OF THE AMERICAN CORNHOLE ORGANIZATION

················

- ▷ Add arc to your throw—and just get the bag on the board.
- ▷ Aim at a mark beneath the hole—your bag will slide.
- ▷ Decide on your throwing stance—and stick with it.
- ▷ Get comfortable with throwing on both sides of the board.
- ▷ Pick your pitch—choose between holding the bag flat, pinched or squeezed into a wad.
- ▷ Have fun and keep a cold beverage close by.

PITCHING STANCES

TRADITIONAL AKA STANDING, REGULAR
By far the most common stance. It allows for less mistakes in player mechanics, but means less drive in the pitch. In this stance, players pitch standing still with either the left or right foot forward for stability.

STEP AKA POWER STEP, HORSEY
Very similar to techniques used in horseshoes. The player takes a step forward while releasing the pitch. The Step is useful in putting additional drive behind a Cornhole pitch but make sure to avoid any foot faults.

SQUAT AKA POP-A-SQUAT, PITCHING A LOAF
This stance is similar to a bodybuilder doing a squat, releasing the bag on the way up. This motion allows for a large arch but can be stressful on the knees.

BREW FACT

An official Cornhole bag is made of fabric that measures six by six inches square and is filled with either two cups of PET resin or two cups of corn feed and then double-stitched. The finished bag weighs roughly one pound.

Dizzy Bat
AKA D-BAT, THE SPINS, LOUISVILLE CHUGGER

Sport, like life, is all about perseverance and overcoming adversity. Sometimes that is battling through an injury or standing up to a Goliath competitor. Sometimes it's battling against self-inflicted vertigo and standing up to an empty can.

WHAT YOU'LL NEED BESIDES BEER

················

❱ 1 plastic bat (aka Wiffle)

SETUP

▷ At least two players are required but a crowd of a hundred screaming lunatics is ideal.

▷ To start, you'll need to cut off the end of the bat's handle and shave or sand it down smoothly so as not to cut your mouth while drinking.

BREW FACT

Dizzy Bat fail videos are running rampant all over the Internet, and—spoiler alert—somebody swings and misses or just falls down in every Dizzy Bat video in history. So if you do post one, make sure someone bites it big time.

GAME PLAY

▷ **POUR.** Empty a can of your favorite beverage into the bat.

▷ **DRINK.** Pretty self-explanatory.

▷ **SPIN.** Orbit yourself around the bat one time for every second it took to drink. (For example, 10 seconds = 10 spins.)

▷ **HIT.** Have your friend toss you the empty can and try to hit it. (Keep repeating until you hit it.)

SCORING (DRINKING) METHOD:

▷ While no points are earned in the game, one does receive the satisfaction of connecting on a hit—and the joy of drinking out of a plastic bat.

▷ Due to the high entertainment value for spectators, beers should be enjoyed by the crowd as well.

Flip Cup

AKA FLIPPY, FLIPPER, TIPPY CUP, TURBO CUPS

Considered Coaster Flipping's little sister and Beer Pong's illegitimate brother-from-another-mother, Flip Cup is arguably one of the hottest beer sports around. The game tests an individual's dexterity and speed as well as the team's ability to function cohesively. The result is copious amounts of smack talk . . . and good times.

WHAT YOU'LL NEED BESIDES BEER

• • • • • • • • • • • • • • •

❱ I plastic party cup per player
❱ I table

SETUP

▷ Two teams with an equal number of players stand on opposite sides of a table directly facing one another.

▷ Teams typically consist of four or more players per side.

▷ One cup is placed in front of each player and filled with a set amount of beer—usually two ounces—at the start of each round.

TEAM A

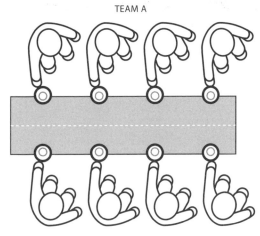

TEAM B

GAME PLAY

▷ **THE TOAST AND THE START:** The game begins with the first two opponents (two players at one end of the table) partaking in a customary toast, which consists of tapping their cups, lowering them down to the table, then raising them back up to the mouth. This marks the start of the round.

▷ **THE CHUG AND THE FLIP:** The players first drink the entire contents of their cups. Once a player's cup is emptied, he must then place the cup mouth-side up on the edge of the table and attempt to "flip" the cup by flicking or lifting the bottom of the cup until it lands mouth-side down. If unsuccessful on the first try, the cup is reset and reflipped until it lands mouth-side down on the table. Players may only use one hand to flip, and cannot blow on or otherwise guide the cup. The next team member cannot touch his cup until the previous player's cup is 100 percent settled and mouth-side down on the table.

▷ **PASS AND REPEAT:** Once the first cup is successfully flipped, the next player in line repeats the same process. This process continues sequentially until all team members have successfully drunk and flipped their cups. In the event that the last two opponents' cups are successfully flipped at the exact same time, the game is decided with a rematch. Flip Cup matches are typically played as a best-of-seven series.

SCORING (DRINKING) METHOD

▷ The victorious team wins the table—staying on to challenge the next team.

▷ The victorious team also wins the chance to drink again during the next match.

MASTERING THE GAME

Proper technique is essential to a successful flip. There are many means to an end but these methods allow for the highest first-flip success rate.

TRADITIONAL WRIST FLICK
AKA SNAKE CHARMER, ALL-IN-THE-WRIST, DEVIL'S HANDSHAKE

With the palm facing up, use the middle and/or index finger to lift the edge of the cup up and slightly forward to complete the flip. Keep the fingers stiff, the wrist nimble, and the mind focused.

FINGER FLICK
AKA TICKLER, STROKE IT, SCRATCHING THE ITCH, TWO-FINGER TANGO

Place just a finger or two to gently lift the bottom of the cup. This flick limits exertion to only the finger muscles — saving all other energy for drinking.

REVERSE WRIST FLICK
AKA SLAPPIN' PAPPY, FORGET-ABOUT-IT, BUZZ OFF

This technique is a bit unorthodox but when performed properly can be lethal and intimidating. With the palm facing away from the cup, place one to three fingertips under the cup's lip. Use both a flick of the wrist and a flick of the fingers to complete the flip.

RULE VARIATIONS

Though Flip Cup's basic rules are practically universal, there are some variations incorporated to spice up the challenge level.

SURVIVOR FLIP CUP
Survivor follows the general rules, except after each match the losing team votes off one player. The remaining players on the team will have to make up for the loss by a player drinking and flipping the voted-off player's cup.

JUNGLE FLIP CUP
Jungle rules mean everyone drinks and flips at the same time. The initial Setup is the same, except the entire table will simultaneously perform the customary toast, then everyone will flip. The first team to have every team member flip their cups wins.

BATAVIA DOWNS FLIP CUP
Players surround a circular table, with opposing players toasting as in the general rules. As each player successfully drinks and flips his cup, the person to his right takes his turn. After each successful flip, players must refill their cups in the event that the player standing directly to the left flips a cup. The game continues as a clockwise race until a player is unable to successfully flip his cup before the person directly to the left flips his.

FLIP CUP TIPS AND TRICKS FROM A PRO
BY MIKE VOLPE, COFOUNDER OF FLIPCUPGUYS.COM

I. Don't swallow. Save time and energy by holding the beer in your mouth while you're flipping. Once you make a successful flip, swallow and enjoy.

2. Treat the cup like a lady. Be polite and gentle and have a delicate touch when flipping. She'll thank you later.

3. Don't wait. Don't let the cup bounce around and finally stop before trying to flip it again. If you know it isn't going to flip, grab it as fast as possible and flip again.

4. Get low. Stand in a crouching position when you're setting up. The closer your lips are to the cup, the faster you can start.

5. Practice, practice, practice! There is no other way to get better at any sport.

Poleish Horseshoes AKA FRISBEER, BEER FRISBEE, BEERSBEE

When you're ready to graduate from basic drinking games, Poleish Horseshoes is the next logical step. Not that balancing beer cans on sticks and whizzing flying objects around is logical, but you get the point.

WHAT YOU'LL NEED BESIDES BEER

••••••••••••••

❱ 2 ski poles
❱ I plastic flying disc (aka Frisbee)

SETUP

▷ Games are played with two teams of two.
▷ The setting requires a soft surface like sand, grass, or even snow.
▷ Stick the two poles upright about twenty to forty feet apart.
▷ Place an empty beer bottle (or can) atop each pole.
▷ Each team chooses one of the poles to stand behind.
▷ Each player *must* have a drink in one hand at all times.

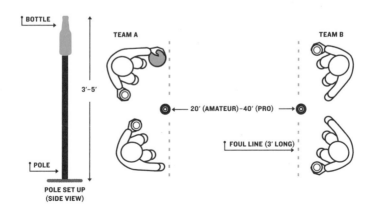

↑ BOTTLE

3'-5'

↑ POLE

POLE SET UP (SIDE VIEW)

TEAM A

TEAM B

← 20' (AMATEUR)–40' (PRO) →

↑ FOUL LINE (3' LONG)

THINGS TO USE FOR A POLE

....

Traditionally, a ski pole is considered the Official Pole of Poleish Horseshoes but there are numerous other things that make a good replacement when one isn't available:

- Broomstick
- PVC tubes
- Plumbing pipe
- Tiki torch (extinguished)
- Fence posts from unfinished project (get off my ass, Mom)
- Abnormally long frozen Hillshire Farms sausages

GAME PLAY

- Teams take turns throwing and catching the disc. Players alternate throwing attempts on each offensive turn. The goal of offense is to knock the empty bottle off the opponents' pole.
- The throwing team must throw the disc so it remains inside the "catching area." The catching area is no more than two steps to the left or right of the pole and no lower than knee height and not so high as to make a player jump. Throws that are outside the catching area are considered "uncatchable" and result in a loss of turn.
- The receiving team must attempt to catch the disc each time it's within the catching area to avoid awarding points to the throwing team. Any player may catch the disc.
- If the bottle is knocked off the pole, either player on the receiving team must catch the bottle before it hits the ground.
- During offense, players must stay behind their pole and during defense, players must wait for the disc to pass the bottle and/or the pole before attempting to catch it.
- Games are played to twenty-one points. Win by two.

SCORING (DRINKING) METHOD

- Uncatchable throw = 0 points and the shooter drinks.
- Disc catch = 0 points and the shooter drinks.
- Bottle and disc catch = 0 points and social—everyone drinks.
- Disc drop = 1 point and the catcher drinks.
- Bottle drop by hitting the pole = 2 points and the catcher drinks.
- Bottle drop by direct hit, aka "dinger" = 3 points and the catcher drinks.
- Drop your drink or no drink in hand = 3 points and replace beer and drink.
- Since a drink in the hand is actually a requirement to the game, casual drinking is clearly part of the game too.

Washers

In England it's called Toad in the Hole, in Hong Kong it's called Holeyboard, and in Hawaii it's known as Potagee, but no matter where it is played, Washers is perhaps the most basic of all beer sports. It makes the perfect entry-level activity into the drinking sports arena. And a handy way to repurpose spare hardware.

WHAT YOU'LL NEED BESIDES BEER

•••••••••••••••

- ❱ 2 milk crates
- ❱ 2 empty coffee cans
- ❱ 4 washers (2 per team)

SETUP

- ▷ Games are typically played outdoors with two teams with two players per team. It can also be played as singles.
- ▷ Two "boxes" must be made (see "Making the Box") and boxes are placed eighteen feet apart.
- ▷ One member from each team stands behind a box.
- ▷ If playing singles, players move to the opposite box for each round.

GAME PLAY

- ▷ Players on the same team stand directly across from one another and stay in this position the entire match. Partners do not stand on the same side or diagonally across from each other (see illustration on next page). If playing singles, both players toss from the same side and switch sides after each turn.

MAKING THE BOX

•••••••••••••••

Place the empty coffee can open end up directly in the center of the milk crate. Secure it to the milk crate with some super-strong glue. It's that easy. Fancy versions can be made using wood, power tools, pipe, paint, and a lot of time, but we've found this milk crate/can version offers the best game play and adds to the aw-shucks character of the sport.

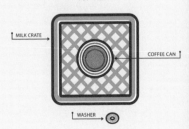

TOP VIEW

MILK CRATE →

COFFEE CAN ↑

↑ WASHER → ◉

▷ Each round, opponents from the same side toss two washers each (one at a time) towards the same opposite box. After each round, play switches to the opposite side.

▷ Players must toss from behind the front edge of the box to avoid a foot fault. A foot fault results in the washer being removed from the box (if applicable). The same rule applies if a player tosses out of turn.

▷ To determines who goes first, one player from each team tosses one washer toward the opposite box and whoever gets closest to or into the can will be the first tosser. This ritual is called the "diddle."

▷ To start the match, the diddle winner tosses both their washers, then their opponent tosses both their washers.

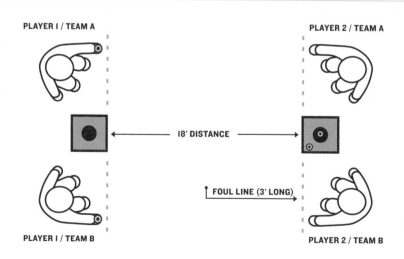

PLAYER 1 / TEAM A   PLAYER 2 / TEAM A

◄— 18' DISTANCE —►

FOUL LINE (3' LONG)

PLAYER 1 / TEAM B   PLAYER 2 / TEAM B

Flipping the washer, like a horseshoe, will result in it bouncing out of control once it hits something. Instead toss it underhand with your thumb and forefinger, like a mini Frisbee, so it "sits" when it hits.

▷ For the remaining rounds, play begins with the player of the team that scored the previous round, always throwing both their washers first.

SCORING (DRINKING) METHOD

▷ A washer that lands inside the crate earns one point.
▷ A washer that lands inside the can earns three points.
▷ A washer that completely misses or bounces off the box and/ or touches the ground results in zero points and the shooter must drink. A foot fault also results in zero points and the shooter must drink.
▷ At the end of each round, the losing side must drink the amount of points they lost the round by.
▷ Just like in Horseshoes and Cornhole, points cancel each other out and only one team can score per round. For example:
  • Team A has one washer in the can (three points) and one washer in the crate (one point) totaling four points.
  • Team B has one washer in the crate (one point) and one washer on the ground (zero points) totaling one point.
  • Team A wins the round scoring three points (four points for Team A minus one point for Team B equals three points net for Team A) and Team B must take three drinks.
▷ The first team to get to twenty-one points wins the game. 13–0 is considered a "washout" and an automatic win. A 17-1 score is called a "whitewash" and also an automatic win.
▷ The losing team must always finish their beers.

SECOND-TIER BEER SPORTS

Just like all sports, there are strata. For every football, there is a curling, hurling, and NHL hockey, important sports that simply don't receive the limelight of their more well-known siblings. But now, this is their time to shine and to bask in the everlasting glory that can only come from inclusion in a few sentences on the last page of a book.

BEERATHALON:

Teams consist of four people, a wooden table, and a wooden bench. Each team member sits on the bench and must consume a full beer. Once everyone is finished, the team gets up and tosses the bench and table as far as they can. Then they sit down and do it again. First team to move fifty yards wins—and nurses their collective hernia.

BEERBALL:

Why should fans be the only ones drinking during a baseball game? No more. A game of softball or baseball is played as usual, with one addition: a full cup of beer is on each base. The runner must consume the contents of the cup before proceeding. Warning: you can hit a home run, but you won't be very safe.

BREWSKEE-BALL:

Skee-Ball with beer. Forget the cheap plastic toys; tickets equal drinks in this hipster hobby. Since it is hard/illegal to bring brews into Chuck E. Cheese's, look online to find local pubs that host Skee-Ball tournaments.

PARTYBALL SOCCER:

The names says it all: soccer with an empty (tap removed) plastic party ball. Same rules as regular soccer, but there's no set field, team structure, penalties, or, really, any similarity to soccer.

COACH SAYS

All right, ladies. You've put in the time to learn about it. Now it's time for you to put down the book and pick up a cup of liquid awesome. But before you do, I need to let you know a thing or two about what I like to call party fouls. Here are a few party fouls a champion should never do. Got it?

- Show up empty-handed
- Screw around with the music
- Spill your beer
- Tell the same dull story over and over again
- Hand out business cards
- Crop-dust through a crowded room
- Clog the toilet
- Fail a keg stand
- Try to start a push-up contest
- Have sex in someone else's bed
- Monopolize the Beer Pong table
- Start a fight
- Finish the last beer
- Finish the last slice of pizza
- Have sex with someone else's bed
- Throw up in a plant
- Run out of beer
- Fail to stand up
- Pass out on the dance floor
- Overstay your welcome
- Pass out with your shoes on
- Piss yourself

BEER BANTER

"Beer is proof that God loves us and wants us to be happy."
—BENJAMIN FRANKLIN

Acknowledgments

CONTRIBUTORS TO BEER AWESOMENESS:

Chris Barish, Michael Ferrari, Frank Geers, Meeko, Ryan Murphy, Porter McKinnon, Derrick Pitman, Mike Student, Tess and Mark Szamatulski at Maltose Express, Mike Volpe, Richard Taylor at TheBeerCast.com, and the National Tailgating League (Chris Dotson, Todd Hirschfeld, Colin Webb).

The authors would like to raise a toast to the entire team at Chronicle Books, especially Emily Haynes and Sarah Malarkey, to our friends at Levine Greenberg, especially Stephanie Kip Rostan and Monika Verma, and to all beer drinkers the world over (snobs not included). We couldn't have done this without you. Cheers!

Ben would like to personally thank: the talented Michael Ferrari (MichaelPFerrari.com) and Ryan Murphy (AskRyanMurphy.com) for their hard work and funny words and my wife for her loving support and free proof-reading. A special shout-out goes to mixed nuts, hot wings, any part of the pig, and conversation with old friends—all for going so damn well with a cold beer.

Dan would like to personally thank: all my beer drinking buddies (you know who you are) for the countless hours of research and development used to make this book; all the basements, bars, pubs, and breweries for putting up with our field-testing; and most of all, much love and thanks to my beautiful wife for putting up with all my shenanigans.